Positive Special Education

Positive Special Education spotlights the power of positive special education, combining insights from researchers and teachers in special education from several countries.

The expert team of authors, being both teachers and academics, highlight the powerful influence of teachers fostering optimistic approaches as well as the impact a positive educational experience has on young students. Instead of focusing on medical perspectives and individual difficulties, this book's uniqueness lies in showcasing how educators, students, and care workers can be empowered to overcome daily challenges by changing beliefs and attitudes. Based on extensive experience in schools across Sweden and the UK, this book:

- contains a history of positive special education and central theoretical concepts such as self-efficacy, implicit theories, and inclusion;
- explores the potential of digital tools and how they can support students with their learning and development;
- focuses on instructional methods in reading, writing, and vocabulary development.

Practical case studies throughout the book provide various examples for educators to apply the principles of positive special education in different learning environments. It is a must-read for teachers in SEND and mainstream schools, in preschool, pre-service teachers as well as undergraduate or masters' students in education.

Monica Reichenberg is Senior Professor at Gothenburg University, Sweden.

Ann-Katrin Swärd is Senior Lecturer at Gothenburg University, Sweden.

Catherine Shipton is Headteacher of Archdale School, Sheffield, UK.

Positive Special Education
Theories, Applications and Inspiration

Edited by Monica Reichenberg,
Ann-Katrin Swärd and Catherine Shipton

LONDON AND NEW YORK

Designed cover image: © Getty Images

First published in English 2025
by Routledge
4 Park Square, Milton Park, Abingdon, Oxon OX14 4RN

and by Routledge
605 Third Avenue, New York, NY 10158

Routledge is an imprint of the Taylor & Francis Group, an informa business

© 2025 selection and editorial matter, Monica Reichenberg, Ann-Katrin Swärd and Catherine Shipton; individual chapters, the contributors

The right of Monica Reichenberg, Ann-Katrin Swärd and Catherine Shipton to be identified as the authors of the editorial material, and of the authors for their individual chapters, has been asserted in accordance with sections 77 and 78 of the Copyright, Designs and Patents Act 1988.

All rights reserved. No part of this book may be reprinted or reproduced or utilised in any form or by any electronic, mechanical, or other means, now known or hereafter invented, including photocopying and recording, or in any information storage or retrieval system, without permission in writing from the publishers.

Trademark notice: Product or corporate names may be trademarks or registered trademarks, and are used only for identification and explanation without intent to infringe.

Published in Swedish by Studentlitteratur AB 2020

British Library Cataloguing-in-Publication Data
A catalogue record for this book is available from the British Library

ISBN: 978-1-032-83398-9 (hbk)
ISBN: 978-1-032-83394-1 (pbk)
ISBN: 978-1-003-50914-1 (ebk)

DOI: 10.4324/9781003509141

Typeset in Galliard
by Apex CoVantage, LLC

Contents

About the editors	*vii*
List of contributors	*viii*
Introduction	*x*

1 What is positive special education?   1
  MONICA REICHENBERG

2 Positive special education: why are teachers' and students' self-efficacy important? Consequences for reading instruction and civic education   7
  MONICA REICHENBERG

3 Special educational consequences of implicit notions of ability   23
  ANNA-CARIN JONSSON

4 An inclusive optimistic approach to inclusion   32
  ELIN LANDE

5 Inviting students to develop their capabilities through narrative   44
  IAN BEARCROFT

6 Digital tools in the classroom   54
  ANN JOHANSSON AND ALEXANDRA KAPPEL

7 Teaching expressive communication to pupils with SEND   63
  GEORGIANA WOODCOCK

8 Teaching functional literacy to pupils with SEN 74
MATT MAGUIRE

9 Inclusive literacy: film, visuals, and creative writing – *The Facts in the Case of Mister Hollow* 85
CATHERINE SHIPTON

10 Using visuals and film to support literacy 96
MELANIE WALKER

11 Positive special education: challenge students to read and write in a creative way without fixed material 103
ANN-KATRIN SWÄRD

12 Learning words and understanding their morphological structures 112
SOLVEIG-ALMA HAALAS LYSTER

13 Using a simple text to develop literacy in an inclusive classroom 124
CAROLYN HARVEY

14 Differentiated teaching 131
OLIVIA CARTER

15 The Witting method – safe, creative, and without textbook 139
LOUISE WRAMNER AND ANN-KATRIN ÅKERMAN

Index 150

About the editors

Monica Reichenberg works as a senior professor at Gothenburg University. Monica Reichenberg's research interests involve reading research, students with intellectual disability, adult education, migration in education, special education, teachers' attitudes, and self-efficacy.

Ann-Katrin Swärd PhD in special education, senior lecturer at Gothenburg university. Her research is broad in the field of special education and today about degrading treatment in preschool. She has for many years also been invited as a guest professor at Hacettepe University, Ankara.

Catherine Shipton has worked with children and young people with special educational needs and disabilities as a teacher, mentor, and senior leader. She is now the headteacher[1] of Archdale School, a special school in Sheffield. She has a particular interest in teacher development and developing pedagogy.

Contributors

Ann-Katrin Åkerman, master of arts. She has taught in municipal adult education at upper-secondary level and at Swedish residential colleges for adult education. She has used the Witting method with students at different levels and with adults. She has trained teachers in the Witting method since the mid-1980s.

Ian Bearcroft is a teacher and has worked with children and young people at primary, secondary, and post-16 age groups. He is based in Sheffield, Archdale School and has a special interest and expertise in working in a multidisciplinary way, with children with autism.

Olivia Carter is a teacher and leader at Swiss Cottage School Development and Research Centre. Olivia has worked extensively in the early years with a range of children with medical and physical needs and moderate to severe learning difficulties.

Carolyn Harvey, now retired, has worked as a teacher, special educational needs co-ordinator, senior leader, and educational consultant in special and mainstream schools throughout her career. She has a particular interest in teaching literacy skills to young people who find learning difficult.

Ann Johansson is working as a special education teacher at compulsory school for students with intellectual disabilities. Ann works also as a senior teacher in the same school developing the school's teaching quality, where digital tools are a part of this development.

Anna-Carin Jonsson, associate professor at Gothenburg University. Her thesis deals with the metacognitive ability to handle different assessments in relation to one's own learning, and test situations are treated. Her research focuses on how beliefs about ability affect students' motivation and learning strategies.

Alexandra Kappel has worked as a special education teacher in compulsory schools for students with an intellectual disability. For more than 20 years she has mainly worked at the upper secondary school, at the elementary school. She is responsible for IT and works to develop the digital tools to be used in teaching.

Elin Lande has 25 years of experience teaching students. She has a master's in special education and school leader education. Lande has been a lecturer for student teachers at Oestfold College. For the last years Lande has been an assistant principal at Tistedal primary school.

Solveig-Alma Halaas Lyster is a professor emerita at Department of Special Needs Education, University of Oslo. Professor Lyster's research focuses on children's language and learning, and she is specifically interested in the nature and causes of children's language and reading difficulties and how best to ameliorate them.

Matt Maguire is the assistant principal for Upper School at Swiss Cottage School Development and Research Centre. Swiss Cottage School has a highly life-skills-based curriculum designed around supporting students to maximise the choice, voice, and independence they have in their lives.

Melanie Walker is a teacher and leader who has worked in London, predominantly with pupils with SEND following a Formal Pathway. Her role has focused on bridging the gap for learners with moderate learning difficulties and mainstream schools.

Georgiana Woodcock has a teacher's degree, gaining experience in both mainstream and primary special schools. Georgiana has taught pupils with autism, moderate learning disabilities, and complex medical needs at Archdale School in Sheffield for four years but teaches now at one special school in Leeds.

Louise Wramner is a special education teacher and BA. She has worked with students with intellectual disability in elementary and secondary schools as well as with adults in a total of 40 years. She has taught illiterate adults with immigrant background for six years.

Introduction

Monica Reichenberg, Catherine Shipton and Ann-Katrin Swärd

The title of our book is *Positive Special Education: Theories, Applications, and Inspiration*. Positive special education is inspired by positive psychology and positive education. Positive special education emphasises the powerful consequences of optimistic beliefs and attitudes in education.

Special needs education has, historically, been dominated by two perspectives. On the one hand a medical perspective that emphasises diagnoses (ADHD, autism, etc.), mental illness, and individual difficulties (inspired by psychiatry), while on the other hand, special needs education has been dominated by critical (arguably cynical) perspectives that highlight marginalisation, constraints, trauma, and oppression of students with disabilities and social problems. In other words, the focus has been somewhat polarised and pessimistic. We read about endless social problems and disrepair without hope and solutions. If you only highlight social problems this fact will lead in turn to a negative view of disability (a self-fulfilling prophecy). We argue for a positive view.

Thus, we contribute with a third perspective that promotes optimism and what teachers and their students can do to mitigate social problems. Although we agree on the importance of social factors, we want to highlight the recent contributions of positive psychology (inspired by the social cognitive and humanistic tradition). Thus, we illustrate how the research on positive special education can guide special education teachers and their students to overcome pedagogical challenges to mitigate social problems (e.g., under-voting of citizens with disability, literacy, access to public transportation).

Although other books on positive education exist, they firstly lack an emphasis on special needs education. This means that other books lack clinical examples from special needs settings and do not converse with special needs research. Secondly, other books on positive education narrowly focus on well-being in affinity with psychology. Although our book shares an emphasis on positive psychology, we offer a perspective closer to social psychological (e.g., self-efficacy, growth mindset) and traditional educational concerns (e.g., civic/democratic education, literacy). In other words, we develop our own take on the topic of positive (special needs) education. Compared to the Swedish edition from 2020, our new book is a significantly elaborated and updated version.

The book was originally a collaboration between Swedish academics and teachers and British teachers at a well-known SEND school in London, bringing theory and practice together. In this new version we have extended our collaboration to a SEND-school in Sheffield, Archdale School.

The contributions of the teachers consist of model lessons aimed to help students develop their self-efficacy in tasks such as literacy and access to public transport. We devote a considerable attention to students with intellectual disability, also referred to as learning disability in the United Kingdom.

The chapters from the UK highlight how to adapt teaching to include a range of pupils, some with the most complex needs, and often through the medium of visual literacy. The book highlights functional and creative ways of doing this. Current chapters include current practice from teachers working within an additional SEND school in the north of the UK and have been informed by the field as well as the background and theories that contributed to the book.

In the book we also highlight central theoretical concepts such as self-efficacy and implicit theories (Chapters 1, 2, and 3). These and other related concepts have been extensively studied in quantitative research (surveys, interventions). However, these research papers often involve technical details that make them difficult to read for teachers. Thus, we hope to communicate the relevance of these concepts to the reader in a non-technical manner while blending them with case studies for practical applications.

The case studies included provide a wealth of examples for how teachers can apply the principles of positive education in their classroom and beyond.

In our different chapters, we will use either intellectual disability or learning disabilities.[2] Learning disability refers to intellectual disability, learning disabilities, and complex needs. Thus, intellectual disability has a more narrow scope, as will be discussed in the book.

Notes

1 A headteacher is the lead professional who has responsibility for a school. This is sometimes referred to as a principal.
2 There are different definitions of disability. Even The United Nations and World Health Organization differ in their definitions. Researchers in disability studies often remind us that the definitions of disability ought to be contested. Although we agree, we nevertheless dodge the debate of the definition and instead focus how we can improve the lives of people with disabilities.

1 What is positive special education?

Monica Reichenberg

Reports of school studies are often negative and focus on what does not work in schools, for example, bullying, dropouts, teacher burn-out, alienation, student failure, gang behaviour, and deviance in general. However, in this book we will highlight the positive, in other words what works in schools, for example, resilience, trust, hope, commitment, and positive behaviour (Hoy & Tarter, 2011). We titled our book *Positive Special Education: Theories, Applications and Inspiration*. Positive special education is inspired by positive psychology and positive education.

Positive special education departs from positive psychology. In this book we use the word psychology synonymously with social psychology.

A common misconception is that positive special education is to be found in the abundant literature of self-help books with positive titles including photos with happy, smiling faces that target children or youths with special needs. Merely putting smiling faces on the cover of some books seldom helps. These self-help books lack evidence-based research.

We have noticed a gap in previous research on positive education/positive special education. This research has overemphasised (a) health outcomes and (b) positive special education experiences but more seldom attended to positive education/positive special education as such. Typically, people misconceive positive special education as positive experiences. On the contrary, positive special education, as we define it, represent optimistic beliefs, as well as capabilities to empower students with special needs and their teachers and mitigate social circumstances. We consider optimistic beliefs and mindsets as both consequences and causes of social circumstances. Therefore, a novelty of our book is that we place a firmer emphasis on the empowering potentials that we consider pivotal for positive special education. Thus, beyond extending the scope of positive special education, we also emphasise the importance of optimistic beliefs such as mindsets and believed capabilities that can empower students in special needs and their teachers. A second novelty to our book is an additional human rights approach to special needs, a capability approach.

DOI: 10.4324/9781003509141-1

In the spirit of Bandura (2011), I will continue by providing a brief introduction to positive psychology and its historical development. Thereafter, I continue with positive education followed by a definition of positive special education and its premises including its applications.

Positive psychology: from *learned helplessness* to learned optimism

The positive psychology perspective was developed by Seligman (Seligman, 2002). Seligman and his colleagues (Seligman 2011, Peterson et al., 1993) discovered that many individuals in some situations showed *learned helplessness*, an expectation that one cannot control important outcomes due to an earlier experience. *Learned helplessness* caused passive behaviour and resulted in people giving up and giving in to stress. They became discouraged, pessimistic about the future, and lacked in initiative. Later, Seligman and his colleagues discovered that people with a high degree of *learned helplessness* tended to score high on three dimensions, or explanatory styles:

1. *Internal:* when students blame themselves rather than the situation, for example, students blaming themselves for poor test results.
2. *Stable:* when students consider bad events as stable (e.g., diseases) as opposed to temporary (e.g., illness). Such is the case when students believe they will always fail instead of thinking that a poor test result may just be due to the student happening to have a "bad day".
3. *Global:* when students generalise and claim that one bad event will have disastrous consequences. Consider the case when students believe that a poor result on a single test will prevent them from getting job or enrol into higher education, that is, a poor test result becomes a catastrophe. The pessimism of catastrophising a single failure can lead to unhealthy behaviours Peterson & Seligman (1984) and Reivich et al., (2023).

Consider the counterfactual, when a student scores low on these three dimensions. A low score on the three dimensions would imply *learned optimism*. Any special educator can promote learned optimism. Consider the case of students with intellectual disability, for example: encourage the students to focus on how they can change the situation, for example, with learning aids, or "blaming" the textbook author (Beck et al., 2020) for not understanding the text.

You can also promote learned optimism by making the students aware that everyone has a "bad day". Highlight that, for example, the best athletes do not always score the goal, however, they focus on their accomplishments (self-efficacy) as opposed to setbacks. Underline that accomplished athletes, politicians, or scientists overcame single challenges, for example, Michael Jordan got benched during high school basketball, and Zlatan Ibrahimović did not became a soccer star overnight. In the next section I will develop the concept of learned optimism further.

Learned optimism

Where does an optimistic or pessimistic belief come from? Some have emphasised the importance of providing children with unconditional positive feedback to promote self-esteem (i.e., feeling happy within oneself). But if children are raised simply feeling good about themselves, they will not be prepared to face challenges and take responsibilities. Researchers have suggested teaching children life skills to bolster genuine self-esteem.

According to Seligman (1991), optimists tend to blame failures on factors that are external, temporary, and specific, and to attribute success to factors that include (a) internal, (b) stable, and (c) global dimensions. Optimism correlates with health. Studies have shown that optimists adopt a problem-focused attitude to coping with stress as opposed to dodging the problem (Nes et al., 2005). In the course of a lifetime, everyone has setbacks. But an optimistic belief helps us to manage and thus overcome challenges. There may even be long-term implications.

Optimistic beliefs and student well-being

Enhancing student well-being originated from the child-centred teaching movements including Montessori, Steiner, and Reggio Emilia (Waters, 2021). Thus, positive education reinforces how teachers that work with an optimistic attitude contribute to "pedagogical wellbeing work" (Pyhältö et al., 2010). Positive education promotes the powerful consequences of optimistic beliefs and attitudes in education (Seligman et al., 2009).

Seligman et al., (2009) argue that skills that increase resilience, positive emotion, engagement, and meaning can be taught to schoolchildren. Teaching these skills could mitigate depression, increase life satisfaction, and work as well as encouraging quality learning and creative thinking. Seligman et al., (2009) successfully replicated the results from positive psychology in an intervention study. The intervention study included a grammar school in Australia that taught the skills of resilience, positive emotion, engagement, and meaning to an entire school. The result supported the claims how these skills result in pedagogical well-being. Although, positive education is still under development, the results seem encouraging in a period of increasing mental illness among young people. Thus, positive education offers an alternative to a medical perspective with its emphasis on disability and diagnoses. The medical perspective will be elaborated further in the chapter by Monica Reichenberg (2024).

Positive special education shares all the ambitions of positive education while expanding the scope to special needs education. Positive special education is inspired by the capability approach/rights-based model. The capability approach emphasises the need to think in terms of capability rather than disability and will be further elaborated in the chapter by Monica Reichenberg (2024).

4 Positive Special Education

From optimistic beliefs to self-efficacy beliefs and growth mindsets

However, positive psychology has been criticised for ignoring realities of life. Bandura (2011) addresses the critics of positive psychology inspired by social cognitive theory. Bandura claims that optimistic beliefs alone do not suffice. Instead, individuals must also believe (have a high degree of self-efficacy) that they can produce the desired effects by their actions. Self-efficacy (directly) affects well-being and satisfaction because it influences the quality of life (directly and indirectly). Self-efficacy is pivotal in positive special education.

Research shows that greater self-efficacy increases your chances that you try harder on a task, persist in the face of failure, and succeed. The implications for mental and physical health are striking. For example, individuals with high self-efficacy on health-related matters are more likely, if they want to, stay physically fit, abstain from smoking, and tolerate pain (Bandura, 1997; Baldwin et al., 2006). People who have a high rather than low level of self-efficacy about their ability to cope with stress also exhibit an enhanced functioning of the immune system (Wiedenfeld et al., 1990).

Sense of coherence beliefs

Positive special education also draws inspiration from the medical sociologist Aaron Antonovsky's (1987) *Sense of Coherence* (SoC). SoC refers to people's confidence in the fact that they can (1) understand, (2) control, and (3) assign meaning to life. These three dimensions can be measured through three corresponding "scales" in questionnaires. The three dimensions have been used in research on health but also research on special education and disability.

SoC helps us understand why people can prosper despite traumatic life events, such as cancer, persecution, or depressions. As long as people can believe they can understand, control, and assign meaning to these life events, they can cope with stress and thus increase their self-rated satisfaction or health. SoC makes people never lose hope and avoid despair or pessimism.

When applied to special education we emphasise SoC to help students or young adults deal with the challenges of learning difficulties, ADHD, autism, seeing, hearing difficulties, etc. SoC can help us understand and explain why some students and young adults overcome tragedies or despair to consider learning difficulties as a life experience and reclaim their dignity.

Antonovsky (1987) emphasised the importance of confidence. We suspect that people with SoC and self-efficacy can avoid *learned helplessness* at a higher probability.

Growth mindsets

Positive special education also draws inspiration from Dweck. Students' mindsets – how they perceive their abilities – play a key role in their motivation and achievement. Students who believed their intelligence could be developed (a growth mindset) outperformed those who believed their intelligence was fixed (a fixed mindset). Mindsets and self-efficacy may be considered as theories of motivation. However, they differ drastically from the everyday notion of motivation (Dweck & Yeager, 2019). A growth mindset means to persuade students that they constantly develop (i.e., "grow"). By implication, a growth mindset means avoiding a fixed mindset ("students do not make progress").

We all fall into a fixed mindset from time to time. However, we should strive to a growth mindset: "struggling is part of learning". However, a growth mindset should not be confused with praising failure. When we care about students, we often praise them for their efforts ("good job"). However, effort does not imply growth. Instead, a growth mindset highlights that challenge is part of the growth and that teachers should aid students to overcome failures.

Outlook of the book

Beyond optimistic beliefs, self-efficacy, mindsets, positive special education also focuses on positive special education models, for example, the Swiss Cottage School Model, which is elaborated in a chapter in this book by Matt Maguire (2024). Self-efficacy will be further developed in the chapter by Monica Reichenberg (2024) and growth mindset in the chapter by Anna-Carin Jonsson (2024) and Ann Johansson and Alexandra Kappel (2024).

Lastly, instead of talking narrowly about inclusion in this book, we talk about participation in school, politics, working life, and leisure.

References

Antonovsky, A. (1987). *Unraveling the mystery of health: how people manage stress and stay well*. (1. ed.) Jossey-Bass.

Baldwin, A. S., Rothman, A. J., Hertel, A. W., Linde, J. A., Jeffery, R. W., Finch, E. A., & Lando, H. A. (2006). Specifying the determinants of the initiation and maintenance of behavior change: An examination of self-efficacy, satisfaction, and smoking cessation. *Health Psychology*, 25(5), 626.

Bandura, A. (1997). *Self-efficacy: The exercise of control*. Freeman.

Bandura, A. (2011). A social cognitive perspective on positive psychology. *Revista de Psicología Social*, 26(1), 7–20.

Beck, I. L., McKeown, M. G., & Sandora, C. A. (2020). *Robust comprehension instruction with Questioning the Author*. Guilford Publications.

Dweck, C. S., & Yeager, D. S. (2019). Mindsets: A view from two eras. *Perspectives on Psychological Science*, 14(3), 481–496.

Hoy, W. K., & Tarter, C. J. (2011). Positive psychology and educational administration: An optimistic research agenda. *Educational Administration Quarterly*, 47(3), 427–445.

Johansson, A., & Kappel, A. (2024). Digital tools in the classroom. In M. Reichenberg, A.-K. Swärd & C. Shipton (Eds.), *Positive Special Education: Theories, Applications and Inspiration* (pp. 54–62). Routledge.

Jonsson, A.-C. (2024). Special educational consequences of implicit notions of abil In M. Reichenberg, A.-K. Swärd & C. Shipton (Eds.), *Positive Special Education: Theories, Applications and Inspiration* (pp. 23–31). Routledge.

Maguire, M. (2024). Teaching functional literacy to pupils with SEN. In M. Reichen A.-K. Swärd & C. Shipton (Eds.), *Positive Special Education: Theories, Applications and Inspiration* (pp. 70–76). Routledge.

Nes, L. S., Segerstrom, S. C., & Sephton, S. E. (2005). Engagement and arousal. Optimism's effects during a brief stressor. *Personality and Social Psychology Bulletin*, *31*(1), 111–120.

Peterson, C., Maier, S. F., & Seligman, M. E. P. (1993). *Learned helplessness: A theory for the age of personal control*. Oxford University Press.

Peterson, C., & Seligman, M. E. (1984). Causal explanations as a risk factor for depression: Theory and evidence. *Psychological Review*, *91*(3), 347–374.

Pyhältö, K., Soini, T., & Pietarinen, J. (2010). Pupils' pedagogical well-being in comprehensive school – significant positive and negative school experiences of finnish ninth graders. *European Journal of Psychology of Education*, *25*(2), 207–221.

Reichenberg, M. (2024). Positive special education: Why are teachers' and students' self-efficacy important? Consequences for reading instruction and civic education. In M. Reichenberg, A.-K. Swärd & C. Shipton (Eds.), *Positive Special Education: Theories, Applications and Inspiration* (pp. 7–22). Routledge.

Reivich, K., Gillham, J. E., Chaplin, T. M., & Seligman, M. E. (2023). From helplessness to optimism: The role of resilience in treating and preventing depression in youth. In S. Goldstein and R.B. Brooks (Eds.), *Handbook of Resilience in Children* (pp. 161–174). Springer International Publishing.

Seligman, M.E. P. (2002). Positive psychology, positive prevention, and positive therapy, in *Handbook of Positive Psychology*, C. R. Snyder & S. J. Lopez (Eds.) (3–9) Oxford University Press.

Seligman, M. E. P. (2011). Building resilience. *Harvard Business Review*, *89*(4), 100–106.

Seligman, M. E. P. (1991). *Learned optimism*. Knopf.

Seligman, M. E. P., Ernst, R. M., Gillham, J., Reivich, K., & Linkins, M. (2009). Positive education: Positive psychology and classroom interventions. *Oxford Review of Education*, *35*(3), 293–311.

Waters, L. (2021). Positive education pedagogy: Shifting teacher mindsets, practice, and language to make wellbeing visible in classrooms. In M.L. Kern and M.L. Wehmeyer (Eds.), *The Palgrave handbook of positive education* (pp. 137–164). Palgrave Macmillan.

Wiedenfeld, S. A., O'Leary, A., Bandura, A., Brown, S., Levine, S., & Raska, K. (1990). Impact of perceived self-efficacy in coping with stressors on components of the immune system. *Journal of Personality and Social Psychology*, *59*(5), 1082.

2 Positive special education

Why are teachers' and students' self-efficacy important? Consequences for reading instruction and civic education

Monica Reichenberg

Some people manage to overcome the most challenging circumstances. Consider the case of Nelson Mandela. The life of Mandela can best be described as a lifetime of struggle against all odds (e.g., apartheid, violence, and imprisonment). Many doubted that Mandela and his peers (ANC) would succeed. "Impossible", the doubters claimed. However, Mandela refused to give up. Despite disbelievers, Mandela never lost confidence in his own or his peers' capability to overcome challenges and setbacks. Thus, Mandela's struggle and wisdom inspired people worldwide to place confidence in their capabilities (Rylander, 2014; Mandela & Langa, 2017).

Confidence in one's capability empowers people. But no child feels confident at birth, rather children learn to believe in their capabilities due to social learning (e.g., inspiration, persuasion, mastery). However, some children learn to doubt their capabilities due to social circumstances. Therefore, we need an education and special education that foster confidence and optimistic beliefs to empower all children and their teachers despite their social circumstances.

This chapter focuses on how we can foster students' and teachers' confidence in their capabilities and its empowering consequences. As examples, I will highlight the consequences of having confidence in our abilities to change with examples from reading instruction, civic and democratic education. Thereafter, I continue with two cases: two models permeated with the optimistic positive special pedagogy I champion. The models, developed by British and Swedish teachers, aim at teaching students how to travel back and forth to school every day. I hope that the models will inspire educators on how to work with young people with intellectual disability (ID).

Throughout the chapter I will argue that self-efficacy, namely, to believe in one's own capability to change through actions (e.g., your teaching when you meet students in difficulties), should be central in positive special education (Bandura, 2008; Seligman et al., 2009). Albert Bandura (whom I introduce later in the chapter) once wrote something in the spirit of Nelson Mandela. Bandura suggested that our self-efficacy beliefs have profound implications for our actions:

DOI: 10.4324/9781003509141-2

Unless people believe they can produce desired effects by their actions they have little incentive to act or to persevere in the face of difficulties.

(Bandura, 2011, p. 8)

However, Bandura underscores the importance of self-efficacy in times of difficulties. All special needs educators and their students know the meaning of difficulties. The optimistic beliefs of overcoming difficulties motivate the importance of self-efficacy.

However, throughout history, these optimistic beliefs have not characterised the views on students with disability. Nevertheless, pessimistic beliefs about the learning capacities of students with disabilities, especially students with ID, have long prevailed in research and teaching in special needs education. Before elaborating on the concept of self-efficacy, I will shortly highlight three views on the learning capacities of individuals with disability: medical, social, and capability views.

From pessimistic to optimistic views on the learning capacities of students with disability

The medical model

> **Concept:** The medical model
>
> Medical views on disability focus on individuals' difficulties. These difficulties are primarily biological and, to a lesser extent, social.

For most of the twentieth century, medical views on disability were predominant. Medical views focus on what individuals with a disability are unable to do, which has led to an underestimation of their skills (Toboso, 2011). By implication, the medical view has reinforced the view of "the able" as superior and the "disabled" as inferior. The medical view has sometimes been called the individual model because the model diagnoses and treats individual learning difficulties. The model insists that individuals' biological dispositions (e.g., genetic, neurological) cause disabilities or special needs (Mitra, 2006; Toboso, 2011; Haegele & Hodge, 2016).

Individuals with a disability have been regarded as care recipients and thus have been treated as objects of medical care (Toboso, 2011). Thus, giving other people the right to decide what is best for them. When it comes to individuals with ID, some people were even terrified of them, and they were placed in institutions to protect other citizens (Toboso, 2011). Contemporary advocates of the medical model can be found in the World Health Organization (WHO, 2001). WHO has a framework – The International Classification of Functioning, Disability and Health, ICF, for measuring health and disability at both individual and population levels. As the functioning and disability of an individual occurs in a context, ICF also includes a list of environmental factors.

The medical model has justified and thus legitimised individuals to be placed in special adapted schools separated from mainstream schools (Toboso, 2011). In teaching there has not been much focus on reading and writing because teachers lacked confidence in the capabilities of their students. However, positive experiences from teaching reading and writing to students with ID have not been missing (see more in Katims [2000] for a historical overview).

Consider the case of Sweden. During Swedish history, many children/ youths with ID have been excluded from education. The line of exclusion has been drawn between the so-called educable and the uneducable. The uneducable were classified as idiots, and there were no expectations that they could develop their capabilities through education. However, we should not consider Sweden as unique. Instead, Sweden represented the prevailing policies accepted by most countries at the time. Swedish children/youths with ID had to wait until 1968 for compulsory education (Persson, 2018).

As a reaction against the medical model, *the social model* was developed in the late 1960s and early 1970s (Mitra, 2006; Toboso, 2011).

The social model

> **Concept:** The social model
>
> Although there are several versions of the social model, all of them agree that disability is caused by restraints and barriers in society.

Several versions of the social model exist. One of them originates from Marxist theory on education and disability (Oliver, 1999). In the Marxist version, capitalism causes disability because capitalists depend on "able" workers, while unable workers do not fit in. Thus, "unable" workers face social exclusion (e.g., discrimination, unemployment, and poverty). Thus, the experience of social exclusion shapes the experience of disability (e.g., "I am disabled"). Therefore, capitalist society must be radically restructured to resolve the problems encountered by people with disability. Similarly, the privatisation of schools, spending cuts, and reduced budgets result in barriers for students with disabilities (Oliver, 1999).

The social constructivist version emphasises the contribution of language. Thus, barriers and limits are a result of language use. For example, the everyday talk of "able" vs. "disabled", "unimpairment" vs. "impairment", "healthy" vs. "unhealthy", and "normal" vs. "deviant" or derogatory terms reflect stereotypes that shape how people treat individuals with ID.

The Nordic version falls under the name of *relational model* (Nilholm et al., 2013). The relational model emphasises the need to focus on the teacher-student relationship as opposed to individuals. Teachers should adopt an attitude that the students do not have special needs but find themselves in a problematic school situation giving rise to special needs. The relational model has similarities with Seligman et al.,'s (2009) argument, developed in the introduction chapter in this book.

When it comes to teaching, it is important that all students remain in the mainstream classroom and not in separate teaching groups outside the classroom. This requires that teachers have a diversity of flexible and supportive teaching strategies and accessible teaching materials.

The social model has been criticised for ignoring the fact that students have often been misidentified and placed in special education when they do not actually have special needs. This is not a social construct but a real fact (Artiles, 2022). In some countries, learners from particular social backgrounds, such as those who are socioeconomically disadvantaged or those from ethnic minorities groups, run the risk of being erroneously labelled as having special needs and thus placed in special education (Artiles, 2022). One approach that takes this into consideration is the capability approach.

The capability approach

Concept: *The capability approach*

The capability approach focuses on the rights of individuals with disability to gain opportunities for developing their capabilities. The approach also wants to change citizens' negative beliefs and attitudes towards individuals with disabilities, rights, and capabilities.

The capability approach underscores that individuals with a disability are not care recipients but individuals with the same needs, rights, and obligations as all other citizens (Pavey, 2003).[1] Therefore, we must assess what individuals are capable of doing rather than accentuating intellectual difficulties or functional limitations (Saleeby, 2007).

The approach advances an optimistic view of disability and special needs and focuses on helping people gain opportunities to independently develop their capabilities (Bigby et al., 2019; Haegele & Hodge, 2016).

The approach underscores how other citizens' negative attitudes and beliefs of people with disabilities disempower students and thus their capabilities (Bigby et al., 2019). Negative attitudes and beliefs include the expression of views such as prejudice, stereotypes (e.g., teachers' low expectations), devaluation, "stigmatisation" (discrediting), and "labelling" (marking).

To counteract negative attitudes in teaching: Teachers have a responsibility to (a) provide students with their rights (e.g., entitlements to special needs); (b) encourage their students to claim their rights in society; and (c) help their students with disabilities gain opportunities to independently solve problems that take place in their everyday experiences; (d) enabling students with intellectual or learning disabilities to continue to use reading, writing, and counting for their own development, get jobs, and participate in society. Thus, teachers need to foster capability rather than disability. Therefore, teachers must work collectively and challenge their own, colleagues', and principals' beliefs and attitudes about their students' capabilities.

On which theory is self-efficacy grounded?

Optimistic beliefs about capabilities can empower students and thus counteract negative beliefs (low expectations, stereotypes, or beliefs about fixed intelligence) and negative attitudes to disabilities or other special needs (e.g., prejudice, devaluations, discrediting). Beliefs about one's capabilities are the essence of self-efficacy. In the next subsections, I will elaborate on the concept of self-efficacy. I start with theory.

Bandura once suggested that:

> we are more heavily invested in the theories of failures than we are in the theories of success.
>
> (Bandura, 1999, p. 215)

In general, I suggest that Bandura's assessment applies to special education, including positive special education. However, Bandura also offers clarification to the concept of self-efficacy.

Self-efficacy rests on social cognitive theory and has been defined as an individual's belief that they are capable of coping with specific tasks. Thus, self-efficacy is not a reflection of an individual's actual skills but rather their beliefs of what they can accomplish with the skills they possess.

If people believe they will be successful in a given task, they are more likely to invest effort, persist in their efforts, and manage upcoming events (Bandura, 1997). Bandura (1997) also proposed that self-efficacy beliefs were (a) self-reflective and (b) powerful motivators of behaviour.

> **Concept:** *Self-efficacy*
>
> Self-efficacy refers to people's belief that they are capable of coping with specific tasks.

Social cognitive theory promotes the belief that human beings can shape their own actions, as a consequence of social learning (Bandura, 1986). In brief, social cognitive theory suggests that people learn from observing others' interactions and from previous experience. Self-efficacy and efficacy expectations are central concepts in this theory.

Bandura (1986) suggested that individuals' beliefs in their own abilities (self-efficacy) influence their values and life choices throughout their life course. According to this theory, people with high self-efficacy are most likely to put their knowledge to use. Teachers' degree of self-efficacy affects the effort teachers invest in their work, and it influences their persistence in the face of setbacks. Self-efficacy beliefs can influence a teacher's choices, efforts, and persistence under difficult conditions. Students' self-efficacy beliefs influence their efforts (a) in the classroom and (b) when performing homework tasks. However, how can we measure an individual's self-efficacy?

How do researchers measure self-efficacy with scales and questionnaires?

Teachers' self-efficacy cannot be defined along a single dimension but has to be defined as multidimensional. Thus, a teacher could have self-efficacy in several dimensions of life. Researchers often use either questions or statements to measure self-efficacy in questionnaires. By grouping and combining similar questions, one may design multiple scales of self-efficacy by subject domain (e.g., reading, mathematics). Commonly, questions/statements about self-efficacy ask "how confident are you to do X?" or "I feel confident that I can do X" or "I can do X", where X represents a concrete task.

In educational sociology, as well as other educational studies, researchers often also measure collective self-efficacy. People's shared beliefs in their collective self-efficacy influence the type of futures they seek to achieve by working together, how well they use their resources (e.g., textbooks, computers, instructional time, faculties), how much effort they invest in their group effort, their perseverance when their efforts fail to produce results or meet opposition, and so on (Bandura, 2011). Collective self-efficacy may be measured by asking individuals to rate their school, class, or neighbourhood about their abilities. Alternatively, one can compute group average self-efficacy by, for example, students in the same classroom or school (Goddard et al., 2000).

Based on Bandura's (1986) conceptualisation of self-efficacy beliefs, Skaalvik and Skaalvik (2007) defined teacher self-efficacy as "individual teachers' beliefs about their own abilities to plan, organize, and carry out activities required to attain given educational goals". Skaalvik and Skaalvik (2011) divided teacher self-efficacy into six aspects that incorporate all the tasks teachers are expected to do: (1) explain and instruct, (2) adapt instruction to individual students' needs, (3) motivate the students, (4) maintain discipline and order, (5) cooperate with parents and other teachers, and (6) cope with changes. According to Skaalvik and Skaalvik (2011), in the context of strategies for teaching reading, self-efficacy refers to a teacher's capability to perform a certain task. Skaalvik and Skaalvik (2007) developed a scale of teacher self-efficacy, Norwegian Teacher Self-Efficacy Scale (NTSES). In this scale, each of the previously mentioned six dimensions contain four questions.

Confidence in one's abilities matters because teachers with greater confidence in their abilities tend to be more successful than those with low confidence in their abilities at a given teaching task. Teachers with greater confidence in their abilities also display greater engagement in the classroom and have greater success at motivating students. When teachers have high engagement and ability to motivate students, they can help students, including those with special educational needs (Copeland & Keefe, 2007; Mojavezi & Tamiz, 2012).

We typically measure self-efficacy as domain-specific knowledge of subjects (e.g., mathematics, reading, writing, civics, physical education) or educator skills (e.g., instructional adaptation, motivating students, managing classrooms). Specifically, educators or students respond to a series of questions or statements about their degree of confidence to master a given task. Examples include the following: "I am confident that I can help students with dyslexia" or "I can motivate students to read". However, self-efficacy can be defined and measured in more general terms: "I can teach". However, as the reader might suspect, general measures of self-efficacy lose precision as teachers may be confident in one domain (e.g., instructional adaptation) but struggle in another (e.g., motivating students to read). Thus, teacher self-efficacy may also depend on the special needs of students. Examples include the following:

I think I am good at teaching students with disabilities.
I think I am good at teaching students with a physical disability.
I think I am good at teaching students with autism.
I think I am good at teaching students with a sensory disability.
I think I am good at teaching students with an intellectual disability.

Thus, one may also discuss self-efficacy in specific school subjects and grade levels. A teacher may have great confidence in their ability to teach civics and read to small children but struggle to teach civics and reading comprehension to youths. Thus, teachers' self-efficacy also depends on the students they teach.

Thus, self-efficacy centres on the individual's belief about what one can achieve or master in a given situation. Thus, self-efficacy cannot be considered a trait (or personality). Self-efficacy has several affinities, including the concept of self-esteem; however, the concept (i.e. self-efficacy) differs from the other concepts (e.g. self-esteem). Social psychologist Rosenberg (1965/2015) developed self-esteem through the inspiration of sociological theories of the self and self-image. Self-esteem centres on one's attitudes towards the "self" (e.g., "I am *satisfied* with myself as a teacher", i.e., self-worth and dignity). However, self-efficacy centres on beliefs and confidence about one's abilities: "I *can* read newspapers". Somewhat simplified, the difference concerns "contentment with oneself" (attitude) vs. "confidence in one's abilities" (beliefs). However, what influences a person's self-efficacy?

What influences a person's self-efficacy?

Bandura (1986, 1997) proposed four (social) sources influencing the extent of an individual's self-efficacy: The first and most powerful source consists of mastery experiences (i.e., prior experiences with given tasks). Success strengthens self-efficacy, whereas repeated failures undermine it; in other words, the belief that teaching has been successful raises self-efficacy expectations that teaching will also be proficient in the future. Self-efficacy beliefs are strengthened substantially when success is achieved on difficult tasks with little assistance or when success is achieved early in learning with few setbacks. The second source consists of vicarious experiences; for example, the target activity is modelled by someone else. We observe others' similar performances of given tasks. Seeing people similar to oneself succeed through perseverant effort raises observers' beliefs in their own abilities. By observing others succeed, we may think, "If they can, I can". The third source consists of verbal persuasion (feedback from others: verbal encouragement and pep talk). Verbal persuasion may also promote a positive perception of potential achievement. Consequently, encouragement from other people – including colleagues – also increases self-efficacy. If people are persuaded to believe in themselves, they will exert more effort. This increases their chances of success. Effective self-efficacy builders do more than convey faith in others. They arrange situations for others in ways that bring success and avoid prematurely placing them in situations where they are likely to fail. They encourage the judgment of success through self-improvement rather than by triumphs over others. Pep talks without guidance achieve little (Bandura, 2011).

The fourth source consists of emotional and physiological states; that is, the happiness level can increase an individual's self-efficacy, whereas stress may have a negative effect on an individual's self-assessed capability (Bandura, 1986, 1997). A stressed individual's negative thoughts and fears regarding their capabilities can decrease self-efficacy and trigger even more stress. Efficacy beliefs are strengthened by reducing anxiety and depression, building physical strength and stamina, and changing negative misinterpretations of physical and affective states. Unless people believe they can produce desired effects by their actions, they have little incentive to act or to persevere in the face of difficulties (Bandura, 2011).

The first and fourth sources of self-efficacy differ: An individual achieves mastery during a longer period. The physiological arousal of self-efficacy is something you get here and now. Teachers need to embrace such opportunities.

To some extent, the degrees of self-efficacy (and its sources) depend on social circumstances such as socio-demographics (e.g., age, neighbourhood, occupation, ethnicity, disability). However, social circumstances can be mitigated by strengthening the self-efficacy of students in need and their teachers.

What are the beneficial consequences of self-efficacy on teachers' work?

Self-efficacy impacts instructional practices, individual and collective efforts among teachers, and persistence within the profession. If teachers believe they will be successful on a given task, they are more likely to be so because they invest substantial effort, persist in their efforts, and manage any negative events (Bandura, 1997). Teachers with a strong sense of self-efficacy perceive that they are able to positively affect student learning and accept responsibility for motivating students and improving their teaching skills until they make progress.

A greater self-efficacy corresponds to greater efforts, which in turn corresponds to improved performance.

Teachers with a high degree of self-efficacy tend to exhibit greater levels of planning and organisation. These teachers are more open to new ideas and more willing to experiment with new methods to better meet their students' needs. They are less critical of students when they make errors, and they work longer with students who are struggling with their reading, for instance. Therefore, these teachers accept responsibility for motivating students and improving their teaching skills until they make progress (Soodak & Podell, 1993; Jerald, 2007).

Teachers with a high degree of self-efficacy are less inclined to refer a difficult student to special education outside the classroom. These teachers will be more likely to retain students with problems in the regular classroom. The better option emphasises quality instruction (e.g., adaption, motivation, classroom management) for students with special needs (Soodak & Podell, 1993; Jerald, 2007). These teachers act on the belief that students with special needs are teachable through extra effort and appropriate instruction (Bandura, 1997). Thus, greater teacher self-efficacy ought to promote a growth mindset among teachers (i.e., all children are teachable and able to learn); the growth mindset is further elaborated on in the chapters by Anna-Carin Jonsson (2024) and Ann Johansson and Alexandra Kappel (2024). One could also consider the mutual influence – for example, when a reading mindset may promote one's reading self-efficacy.

Teachers with greater self-efficacy believe they can mitigate "neighbourhood effects" (due to, e.g., poverty, crime rate, unemployment). Instead, these teachers believe they can act as role models for their students. Although many schools struggle with disengaged parents, teachers with greater self-efficacy refuse to rest in their attempts to engage parents. These teachers believe they can engage parents in the following: their children's homework, attendance at parental meetings, or participation in other school activities. In other words, self-efficacy helps teachers to act in spite of social problems (e.g., neighbourhood effects, parental disengagement; Bandura, 1997).

Teachers with a low degree of self-efficacy do not expect themselves to be successful in teaching students with difficulties. Consequently, these teachers put forth less effort in the preparation and delivery of instruction, and they give up easily at the first sign of difficulty, even if they actually know about strategies that could assist these students if applied. These teachers believe there is little they can do if students are unmotivated (Bandura, 1997). Self-efficacy beliefs can therefore become self-fulfilling prophecies, validating teachers' beliefs of either capability or incapacity (Merton, 1948).

For example, Guo et al., (2012) found that teachers' self-efficacy predicted their classroom practice. In turn, classroom practice predicted student learning and achievements. Thus, teachers' self-efficacy matters in schools and in society at large.

How can teachers support the development of students' self-efficacy?

As mentioned in the introduction, Bandura (2011) claimed that it is not enough that the teachers encourage students to embrace optimistic beliefs in order to perform a task. The teachers must also persuade students that the task is doable and that their intentions can produce the desired effects by means of their actions. Bandura (1986) suggested structure and goal orientation to make the task doable for students. Moreover, the goals have to be explicitly formulated and realistic. There are sub-goals and long-range goals. Short-term sub-goals focus on what has to be done in the here and now in order to make a distal vision a reality. By attaining sub-goals, students build up a belief in their self-efficacy from ongoing advancement towards what they value rather than suspending satisfaction until they fulfil the long-range goal they have set for themselves (Bandura, 2011).

Thus, teachers need to adapt their teaching tasks so that they pose a doable challenge for students. If students believe they can master the task, there is a chance they will also engage with more challenging tasks. Schools can make substantial difference in the student's experience of task difficulties by adapting the instruction to a level that improves their perceived chances of succeeding with the task. If teachers can make students believe they can succeed, they will address one of the factors behind student self-efficacy (see Andreassen & Reichenberg, 2018).

We investigated how the degree of self-efficacy influences teachers' reading instruction (Reichenberg & Andreassen, 2019). In our study, Swedish and Norwegian teachers participated. We found that teachers with a high degree of self-efficacy were very structured in their reading instruction. They were more likely to read aloud to their students, let them talk about texts, and conduct teacher-guided text talk in small groups. In other words, they practised reading activities that have proven advantageous in developing students' reading comprehension. How can teachers encourage students to develop their self-efficacy in civic and functional literacy, for example? This will be highlighted in the next section.

How can teachers' self-efficacy influence the teaching and outcomes of civic education?

The aim of teaching in civic education is to enhance knowledge about the foundations of society, including governance and political institutions, regimes, and civil society. In the beginning of the twentieth century, educational philosopher Dewey (1999[1916]) noted that democracy education (today we most use the concept civic education) was the main objective of school.

Voting is an important part of political citizenship. Allowing citizens to elect who should represent them is the hallmark of electoral democracy. All votes count equally in a democracy, as one of the participants with an ID in the study of Agran et al., (2016) stated, "My vote counts too". However, if some demographics in the population no longer vote at the same rate as the whole population, the electoral system will lose its legitimacy. Primary barriers to voting for people with ID are the negative attitudes of others around them, such as family members and disability support staff, and legal provisions that exclude or excuse them from voting (Bigby et al., 2019; Potocnik, 2019).

Encouraging voting behaviour among people with ID is an important matter of democracy. The power of a democracy rests on its capacity to represent all people, including people with ID (Redley, 2008; Schriner et al., 2000).

In Sweden, citizens with disabilities have a lower electoral participation compared to those without (Statistics Sweden, 2023). Similarly, in the United Kingdom, the participation has been low. However, in an intervention study, people with ID were encouraged to vote and offered practical support on the election day. There were statistically significant increases in both the proportion of individuals registered and in the proportion who voted (James et al., 2021).[2]

Teachers can make a difference by working towards enhanced self-efficacy in civic education. In an inclusive education, all students should be prepared for their participation in elections and thus encouraged to make their voices heard (the capability/rights-based approach of disability). In other words, teachers can encourage students to develop their political self-efficacy (e.g., "I can influence politics by voting", "I can participate in political discussions").

In a study we found that attitudes towards encouraging voter behaviour is associated with special educators' self-efficacy as special educators. Special educators who feel that they have mastered the inclusion of students with ID contribute to a greater propensity of positive attitudes towards encouraging voting behaviour (Reichenberg & Löfgren, 2019). Beyond civic engagement, students must be able to use public transports to be active citizens. Using public transports require students to master functional literacy. I will elaborate on this in the next subsection.

How can teachers' self-efficacy influence teaching in functional literacy? A positive Swedish example

Several students travel to school with special needs transportation services (e.g., buses that operate like cabs). However, without access to the services, students must take responsibility for their own transportation to school or leisure activities. Thus, if students with ID have the ability to travel to school by themselves, their independence will increase.

Unfortunately, many students with ID have little confidence in their capability to travel to school on their own. What is more, parents are more likely to believe their children with ID are unable to travel to school on their own. Usually, parents of children with a disability are too overprotective (Hohlfeld et al., 2018). If parents are overprotective, it becomes more important that the staff encourage students to strengthen their self-efficacy so that they are confident to travel to school on their own.

In line with the capability approach/right-based model, British and Swedish teachers have developed two models aiming at teaching students how to travel back and forth to school every day. Intertwined in the models is functional literacy. Functional literacy views reading as a social practice. Enhancing functional literacy can be a potential strategy for helping students to improve their self-efficacy.

In Chapter 8 of this book, Matt Maguire (2024) describes the Swiss Cottage School model on how to travel back and forth to school by underground. I will here describe a model that has evolved as a result of close cooperation between the staff, students, and parents. Inspired by the capability approach, the staff offer the students opportunities to develop their capabilities. The responsible teacher, and the assistants start with introductory training that includes questions like, (a) what do we do when we travel by bus, (b) how do we get on the bus, (c) what do we do with our tickets, (d) where do you show your ticket, (e) how do we get off the bus, and (f) how do we tell the bus driver that we want to get off the bus at the next stop? By asking these questions, the teacher helps the student form expectations and build confidence that is triggered each time they travel by bus. In addition, the teaching staff review the traffic rules together with their students. Here, the teaching staff make good use of digital devices (e.g., smartphones, tablets, smart boards). Thus, teachers, students, and their assistants watch videos, and together with their parents, the students use smartphone apps such as Find My Device.

When the introductory training is finished, the entire class travels together by bus. Then, the individual training with school assistants begins. Each school assistant is in charge of one to two students. In the classroom, the teacher teaches bus training to students for them to use while outside the classroom.

When riding the bus, students practise using their bus passes and notifying the bus driver when they want to get off the bus. Students practise until they are able to use the bus pass independently. The assistant uses visual support, which includes video recording the students in different situations. The assistant edits the recordings into a coherent story. Later, students can watch the recordings repeatedly. Initially, students need considerable help from their assistants; however, with time, they gradually become more independent. Nevertheless, the assistant never leaves the student to function on their own. The assistant monitors their progress and assists if needed. Once the student feels confident enough to ride the bus independently, the assistant hides and observes them from a distance. When the assistant concludes that the student can ride the bus on their own, they stop following them. However, the student is required to notify the assistant that "I am taking the bus" using their smartphone.

Afterwards, the student walks from their residence to the bus stop or transit station, where an assistant awaits them. After school, the student takes the lead and guides the assistant to the bus stop or transit station. After repeating the procedure multiple times, and once the assistant feels confident that the student can walk alone without a "guardian" awaiting them, they are allowed to travel by bus independently. However, the student is never left completely alone as the assistant hides out of sight to determine if they have safely boarded the bus. The school and parents communicate by phone during the bus ride. As soon as the student gets off the bus, they call the assistant. The duration of the procedure varies according to the student's abilities.

The examples demonstrate how teachers and school assistants can make a difference by encouraging students with ID to develop their self-efficacy: "I can learn to go by bus on my own". The British and Swedish teachers encourage their students to have confidence in their capabilities. Becoming an independent traveller is a great source of pride for young people's confidence and autonomy. If students are trained in school to actively participate in the community, they will be better equipped when they leave school. On the contrary, if students with ID are not trained in school to participate in community activities, they risk social isolation and thus marginalisation. Community activities offer additional benefits such as companionship, support, and development (emotional, social, and cognitive). Thus, special educators need to encourage participation in community activities which expand students' social networks and thus counteract social isolation.

Summary

In this chapter I have argued for the importance of promoting optimistic approaches to learning difficulties (i.e., to think in terms of capability rather than disability).

Following Bandura (1986), I have underlined the importance of both teachers and their students developing their self-efficacy in various domains such as (a) civic education, (b) functional literacy, and (c) independence in transportation (e.g., travelling on the bus on their own). Strengthening these domains will promote participation in society (e.g., education, politics, work, and leisure activities).

People develop self-efficacy due to social factors: (a) vicarious experiences, such as observations and role models; (b) mastery, such as life experiences of accomplishments (e.g., having won a game of soccer or chess); (c) persuasion, such as successful encouragement; and (d) emotions triggered by life experiences (e.g., positive and negative appraisals).

By implication, teachers and parents must foster students' confidence in their own capabilities and focus on students' accomplishments rather than their failures. Fostering capabilities include (a) encouragement of students' believed capabilities and (b) ensuring opportunities for students to develop their capabilities.

Beyond students, parents and teachers must also develop their own self-efficacy. As with students, the same factors develop parents' and teachers' self-efficacy. Thus, parents and teachers need role models, persuasion, and exposure to successes as opposed to failures. For example, successful athletes at the Olympics typically report that they focus on what went right as opposed to what went wrong. These athletes also have coaches that encourage them in a convincing manner (as opposed to a mere "pep talk") and teach them how to practise self-persuasion (e.g., "I am confident in my skills", "I do not care about others"). Such strategies can also be successfully used as part of a positive special education.

Acknowledgements

This chapter was originally published in Swedish in 2020. The English chapter has been fully revised to accommodate to an international readership.

Notes

1 Initially, the economist and Nobel Prize laureate Sen developed the capability approach (Mitra, 2006). Later, the approach has then been adapted and applied to disability research. Researchers sometimes refer to the approach as the right-based model (Burchardt & Vizard, 2014).
2 An inspiring example was reported in *The Guardian*. Mar Galcerán has made history as Spain's first parliamentarian with Down's syndrome | Spain | *The Guardian* (January 9, 2024).

References

Agran, M., MacLean Jr, W. E., & Andren, A. K. (2016). "My voice counts, too": Voting participation among individuals with intellectual disability. *Intellectual and Developmental Disabilities*, 54(4), 285–294.
Andreassen, R., & Reichenberg, M. (2018). Svenske og norske læreres forventninger om å mestre elevtilpasset leseopplæring: Betydningen av lærernes praksiserfaring og andre lærer- og skolerelaterte variable [Swedish and Norwegian teachers' self-efficacy for differentiated reading instruction: The importance of practice and other teacher and school-related variables]. *Nordic Studies in Education*, 3(38), 232–251.
Artiles, A. J. (2022). Interdisciplinary notes on the dual nature of disability: Disrupting ideology–ontology circuits in racial disparities research. *Literacy Research: Theory, Method, and Practice*, 71(1), 133–152.
Bandura, A. (1986). *Social foundations of thought and action: A social cognitive theory*. Prentice Hall.
Bandura, A. (1997). *Self-efficacy: The exercise of control*. Freeman.
Bandura, A. (1999). A sociocognitive analysis of substance abuse: An agentic perspective. *Psychological Science*, 10(3), 214–217.
Bandura, A. (2008). An agentic perspective on positive psychology. In S. J. Lopez (Ed.), *Positive psychology: Exploring the best in people, Vol. 1. Discovering human strengths* (pp. 167–196). Praeger Publishers/Greenwood Publishing Group.
Bandura, A. (2011). A social cognitive perspective on positive psychology. *Revista de Psicología Social*, 26(1), 7–20.

Bigby, C., Tipping, S., Bould, E., & Thiele, R. (2019). *Final report: Strategies to support people with intellectual disabilities to participate in voting*. Living with Disability Research Centre, La Trobe University.

Burchardt, T., & Vizard, P. (2014). 'Operationalizing' the capability approach as a basis for equality and human rights monitoring in twenty-first-century Britain. In *Human rights and the capabilities approach* (pp. 91–119). Routledge.

Copeland, S. R., & Keefe, E. B. (2007). *Effective literacy instruction for students with moderate or severe disabilities*. Brookes Publishing Company.

Dewey, John (1999[1916]). *Democracy and education: An introduction to the philosophy of education*. [New ed.] Free Press.

Goddard, R. D., Hoy, W. K., & Hoy, A. W. (2000). Collective teacher efficacy: Its meaning, measure, and impact on student achievement. *American Educational Research Journal, 37*(2), 479–507.

Guo, Y., Connor, C. M., Yang, Y., Roehrig, A. D., & Morrison, F. J. (2012). The effects of teacher qualification, teacher self-efficacy, and classroom practices on fifth graders' literacy outcomes. *Elementary School Journal, 113*(1), 3–24.

Haegele, J. A., & Hodge, S. (2016). Disability discourse: Overview and critiques of the medical and social models. *Quest, 68*(2), 193–206.

Hohlfeld, A. S., Harty, M., & Engel, M. E. (2018). Parents of children with disabilities: A systematic review of parenting interventions and self-efficacy. *African Journal of Disability, 7*(1), 1–12.

James, E., Hatton, C., & Mitchell, R. (2021). Participation of learning disabled people in the parliamentary election of 2019 in the United Kingdom. *Tizard Learning Disability Review, 26*(2), 65–72.

Jerald, C. D. (2007). *Believing and Achieving (Issue Brief)*. Washington, DC: Center for Comprehensive School Reform and Improvement.

Johansson, A., & Kappel, A. (2024). Digital tools in the classroom. In M. Reichenberg, A.-K. Swärd & C. Shipton (Eds.), *Positive Special Education: Theories, Applications and Inspiration* (pp. 54–62). Routledge.

Jonsson, A.-C. (2024). Special educational consequences of implicit notions of abil In M. Reichenberg, A.-K. Swärd & C. Shipton (Eds.), *Positive Special Education: Theories, Applications and Inspiration* (pp. 23–31). Routledge.

Katims, D. S. (2000). Literacy instruction for people with mental retardation: Historical highlights and contemporary analysis. *Education and Training in Mental Retardation and Developmental Disabilities, 35*(1), 3–15.

Maguire, M. (2024). Teaching functional literacy to pupils with SEN. In M. Reichenberg, A.-K. Swärd & C. Shipton (Eds.), *Positive Special Education: Theories, Applications and Inspiration* (pp. 70–76). Routledge.

Mandela, N., & Langa, M. (2017). *Dare not linger: The presidential years*. Pan Macmillan.

Merton, R. K. (1948). The self-fulfilling prophecy. *The Antioch Review, 8*(2), 193–210.

Mitra, S. (2006). The capability approach and disability. *Journal of Disability Policy Studies, 16*(4), 236–247.

Mojavezi, A., & Tamiz, M. P. (2012). The impact of teacher self-efficacy on the students' motivation and achievement. *Theory & Practice in Language Studies, 2*(3), 483–491.

Nilholm, C., Almqvist, L., Göransson, K., & Lindqvist, G. (2013). Is it possible to get away from disability-based classifications in education? An empirical investigation of the Swedish system. *Scandinavian Journal of Disability Research, 15*(4), 379–391.

Oliver, M. J. (1999). Capitalism, disability and ideology: A materialist critique of the normalization principle. In R. J. Flynn & R. A. Lemay (Eds.), *A quarter-century of normalization and social role valorization: Evolution and impact* (pp. 163–173). University of Ottawa Press. http://www.independentliving.org/docs3/oliver99.pdf

Pavey, B. (2003). Citizenship and special-educational needs: What are you going to do about teaching them to vote? *Support for Learning, 18*(2), 58–65.

Persson, M. (2018). *Gamla synsätt spökar än-funktionshinder genom tiderna* [Old views on disability are still there]. Instant förlag.

Potocnik, M. (2019). *Excluding citizens with disabilities from voting challenging barriers in Australia. A discussion paper from the Centre for Welfare Reform. Australia.* Excluding Citizens with Disabilities from Voting (citizen-network.org).

Redley, M. (2008). Citizens with learning disabilities and the right to vote. *Disability & Society, 23*(4), 375–384.

Reichenberg, M., & Andreassen, R. (2019). Self-efficacy as a predictor of reading instruction: A comparison between Norwegian and Swedish teachers. *L1 Educational Studies in Language and Literature, 19*, 1–29.

Reichenberg, M., & Löfgren, K. (2019). The puzzle of low voter turnout: On the association between Swedish special educators' self-efficacy for inclusive education and attitudes toward encouraging pupils with intellectual disability to vote. *Citizenship Teaching & Learning, 14*(1), 67–85.

Rosenberg, M. (1965/2015). *Society and the adolescent self-image.* Princeton University Press.

Rylander, S. (2014). *Nelson Mandela: tolerans och ledarskap.* [Nelson Mandela: Tolerance and leadership]. Historiska media.

Saleeby, P. W. (2007). Applications of a capability approach to disability and the international classification of functioning, disability and health (ICF) in social work practice. *Journal of Social Work in Disability & Rehabilitation, 6*(1–2), 217–232.

Schriner, K., Ochs, L., & Shields, T. (2000). Democratic dilemmas: Notes on the ADA and voting rights of people with cognitive and emotional impairments. *Berkeley Journal of Employment and Labor Law, 21*(1), 437–472.

Seligman, M. E., Ernst, R. M., Gillham, J., Reivich, K., & Linkins, M. (2009). Positive education: Positive psychology and classroom interventions. *Oxford Review of Education, 35*(3), 293–311.

Skaalvik, E. M., & Skaalvik, S. (2007). Dimensions of teacher self-efficacy and relations with strain factors, perceived collective teacher efficacy, and teacher burnout. *Journal of Educational Psychology, 99*(3), 611–625.

Skaalvik, E. M., & Skaalvik, S. (2011). Teacher job satisfaction and motivation to leave the teaching profession: Relations with school context, feeling of belonging, and emotional exhaustion. *Teaching and Teacher Education, 27*(6), 1029–1038.

Soodak, L. C., & Podell, D. M. (1993). Teacher efficacy and student problem as factors in special education referral. *Journal of Special Education, 27*(1), 66–81.

Statistics Sweden (SCB). (2023). *Voter turnout in the general elections 2022.* Retrieved from https://www.scb.se/publication/50826?menu=open

The Guardian. Mar Galcerán has made history as Spain's first parliamentarian with Down's syndrome | Spain | *The Guardian* (January 9, 2024). Retrieved from https://www.theguardian.com/world/2024/jan/09/mar-galceran-makes-history-spain-first-parliamentarian-downs-syndrome

Toboso, M. (2011). Rethinking disability in Amartya Sen's approach: ICT and equality of opportunity. *Ethics and Information Technology, 13*, 107–118.

World Health Organization (WHO). (2001). International classification of functioning, disability and health. Retrieved from https://www.who.int/standards/classifications/international-classification-of-functioning-disability-and-health.

3 Special educational consequences of implicit notions of ability

Anna-Carin Jonsson

As a teacher it is important to understand what beliefs you carry with you, as these will affect the work both in the classroom and in the individual meeting with a student. This chapter concerns our notions of what we believe ability to be, as this shifts over time, place, culture, as well as between individuals. What do you personally consider ability to be?

Implicit theories of ability deal with people's notions of their own ability to learn. The reason for calling these concepts "implicit" is because they are related to other complex systems of meaning that humans create. A person's opinion or theory of what ability is does not necessarily have to be the same as the scientific theories. A student's implicit theory of ability has been shaped by the student's personal experiences in their own culture in interaction with family, friends, classmates, teachers, the media, and so on (Dweck, 1999). I will focus here solely on the implicit theories that people have about the concept of ability (which is used here synonymously with the concepts of "mindsets" or "intelligence" from Carol Dwecks' research).

Implicit theories of ability mean that a student has formed an idea of what ability is and that this notion influences the student's actions in different learning situations. If the student assumes that ability can be developed by simply working on the task, the student will put in a little more effort and continue to work on the task (even if the student does not understand the task initially). And this is important, to keep trying, continue the work on the problem area itself, will drive development and raise the skills of the student. The student, on the other hand, based on the notion that ability is something fixed that he/she lacks, can make the rational decision that it is unnecessary to waste one's energy when one lacks this ability. After all, it makes no sense to persevere with a task – to put more energy into it – if you lack the tool to solve it, in this case the "ability" tool. From this point of view, to put time and effort into something that is unreachable would be highly irrational.

Carr and Dweck (2011) argue that implicit theories of ability are closely related to students' perceptions of the "self" and identity processes. They capture the student's perception of the opportunity to develop and change. Students who harbour a stronger notion that ability is something fixed and inborn feel that the tests and diagnoses used by the teachers will generate evidence of whether they have the ability to learn or not, for example, the ability to learn to read or learn math (De Castella & Byrne, 2015). This attitude can cause a decline in confidence in one's own ability if students interpret a poor result on a test as proof that they do not have the ability. Dweck (1999) believes that it is very important that teachers take on the responsibility of clearly marking that if the student completes all the tasks without a single error, then the teacher has failed. If the student already knows everything, there is nothing more to learn. It is natural for students to make mistakes. Errors that occur during learning give the student a real chance to learn something new – that they don't already know. If the student only receives questions that they already know the answer to, the opportunity becomes only pure repetition. In other words, implicit theories of ability seem to influence individuals' learning strategies (Dweck, 1986; Carr & Dweck, 2011) and their cognitive performance (Cury et al., 2006). Furthermore, how well they do in school (Blackwell et al., 2015) and what learning outcomes the student, teacher, and classroom as a collective embrace and work from (Middleton & Midgley, 1997; Patrick et al., 2011).

Implicit theories of ability also influence students' self-image, identity, purposefulness, motivation, the challenges they are willing to accept, the effort they will put in, and the tenacity they exhibit when confronted with difficulties (Blackwell et al., 2015; Dweck & Master, 2009). Depending on what view of ability the student has, the student will deal with failures in different ways. If the student believes that ability is fixed and immutable, this can lead to negative effects on learning and motivation. A view of ability as developable instead provides the conditions for positive effects on learning and motivation. I shall therefore describe the two theories in more detail in the next section.

Notions of ability as fixed or changing

"Entity theories of intelligence" or "fixed mindsets" refer to the notion that ability is a property, a fixed feature of the individual as a character, something one has or does not have and that is fixed, inborn, and immutable (Dweck, 1999). If the student in his/her school work starts from this theory, this can have negative effects on learning for several reasons. If the student is convinced that ability is a fixed characteristic inside the student himself, then the result on each task, test, and accounting will be a proof of what the student is. This is problematic for learning as it arouses fear/anxiety about the evidence of appearing as an "approved" student/person. This theory, which is characterised by the notion that the human being is born with fixed properties, is linked to the identity of the student, to the self, something that one is or is not and cannot do anything about. A "self" that all people naturally want to experience as something positive. Carr and Dweck (2011) argues that the effects of entity theories are closely related to self and identity processes. For example, if you have failed and answered incorrectly, you see this as proof of what you are, what the self contains – in this case, proof of something negative about the self, that you are incompetent. Thus, various defence mechanisms are brought to life, which in turn generate strategies of avoidance and helplessness (De Castella & Byrne, 2015). In other words, students avoid tasks where they risk failing, as this creates anxiety and psychological pain because they see the failure as proof of their own incompetence or stupidity. This approach takes energy from the students, energy that could instead be used to try to solve the task (Blackwell et al., 2015). Those students who make use of this theory of ability as something innate and unchanging to a greater extent choose simple well-known tasks that will not generate a challenge in their learning. Students can also give up or seek out areas other than school where they can gain appreciation (Dweck, 1999), an appreciation that, however, in the longer term does not help them develop the competencies they need to be able to orient themselves in society. It is important to notice that a student who interrupts the activity earlier when they note that because "I" do not understand something, the "I" lacks the ability, it is therefore pointless to spend more time on the task. The important conclusion we can draw from this is that how students understand themselves and their own abilities will affect performance (Dweck & Yeager, 2019).

"Incremental theories of intelligence" refers to the notion that ability is changeable, dynamic, and can evolve in the course of work (Dweck, 1986; Dweck, 1999). If the student assumes that ability is something that can be practised, that is, the more you try and persevere, the more you develop, the student will interpret failures in study situations in a different way. If you fail an assignment or an exam, it is not that you lack ability but that you have not worked enough on it. Making more or less of an effort is seen as something you can regulate to a greater extent, unlike an ability you either have or don't have: "I didn't study for the exam, but if I really had put in the time and studied, it would have gone better". This de-dramatises the failure itself as it is no longer an inner characteristic that can be revealed. The student dares to take on new unknown tasks without worrying about whether he/she will succeed or fail, as this is not linked to how the student "is". Since the student does not need to activate various forms of defence of the self, he/she can put energy into the task in question. The most important thing will not be the goal but the way, which involves learning something you could not before (Dweck, 2012). This creates better conditions for the student to learn. If the student assumes that ability is developable and dynamic, that failures are not proof that one does not have the ability to learn but instead a natural part of all learning. Here the student will hopefully seek to focus on the fact that "the more I work on the task and try to understand, the more I will develop". This will have positive consequences on the student's motivation, progression, and performance (Blackwell et al., 2007; Blackwell et al., 2015).

Implicit theories about ability are influenceable

Numerous studies have shown that the same person will estimate their view of ability differently depending on which school subject (for example, mathematics, English, or social studies) the assessment itself relates to. In general, it is the subject of mathematics that stands out, where both students and teachers seem to have a stronger confidence that ability in mathematics is something innate, fixed, and genetic, while in social studies, for example, a more dynamic view of ability is preferred (Mascret et al., 2015). It has also been shown that students are influenced by the extent to which they are exposed to a discipline such as mathematics. Together with Dennis Beach I showed that students from different programmes in year 1 of the Swedish upper secondary school did not differ in terms of their notions of ability as fixed. But in third grade, the students at the science programme had a stronger notion of ability as fixed compared to the students in the social science programme (Jonsson & Beach, 2017).

How implicit theories of ability can be influenced by feedback

Giving appreciative feedback to students has generally been seen as a positive reinforcement in the student's learning and as a stimulus to motivation (Rathel et al., 2008). However, this seems to be a somewhat simplistic picture. Henderlong Corpus and Lepper (2002, 2007) showed that different types of feedback that the researchers gave to the participating children in the study had different results. A certain kind of feedback can stimulate motivation and the desire to learn more, while another type of feedback can rather have negative consequences. The distinction exists between praising the person or praising the learning process itself. Dweck (1999) argues that when teachers focus on praising the process itself, that is, that the student has tried, they also reinforce the confidence that ability is something that is dynamic, that can be developed by the student trying and trying again. If, on the other hand, the teacher uses feedback that focuses on the person, that is, that someone is smart or good, they reinforce the belief that ability is something that exists or does not exist within the individual, which they have or do not have. This can have negative consequences for the student's self-concept, motivation, and performance.

Pre-schoolers with the distinct view that ability is fixed chose again and again the simplest puzzle of six of varying degrees of difficulty and succeeded again and again – but did they learn anything (Dweck & Legget, 1988). This is where we come to more constructive feedback, which means directing the feedback on the effort the children put into the task which can lead to increased learning and greater achievement (Henderlong Corpus & Lepper, 2002; Jonsson & Beach, 2012). If you as a teacher say, "Great that you worked so hard with this difficult task!" in that you give a positive response that the child or young person has tried. It is important to praise learning itself as such and seek to stimulate this instead of short-term successful results.

In special education it can be extra important to consider these beliefs in students, that is, if they believe that their ability can be developed and is dynamic or if they assume that it is not influenceable – that it is something they have or lack. Dweck (1999) argues that groups that are exposed to different types of stereotypical threats from society, such as the stereotype of "possessing" a lower ability than other people, can undermine their own performance. One defines oneself as a person with a low "quantity" of a fixed ability and initially assumes that one will not be able to perform on various tasks. These students do not give themselves the chance to develop their potential as it could be developed and avoid challenges where they risk failure. However, Carr and Dweck (2011) argue that this threat can be alleviated if one seeks to build up notions that ability is dynamic and developable in the student.

Another problem is that in many countries there have been traditions within the school system of dividing students according to expected ability (Kaufman, 2013; Nisbett, 2009). This does not necessarily mean in physical classrooms/classes (although this occurs) but how the school generally categorises students, for example, with a diagnosis or without. In doing so, the very expectation of student learning is categorised (Rosenthal & Jacobson, 1992). These expectations, based on categories such as high and low achievers, are expressed in the *self-fulfilling prophecy* – which means that, for example, the tasks and challenges offered to the student are determined by the teacher's expectations of the category in which the teacher has placed the student.

The consequence is that some students are not offered the tasks and challenges that could lead to their development, as they are already defined to belong to a low-ability category. The teacher then seeks to meet up with assignments adapted to the imagined category instead of with tasks that can challenge and develop the individual student (Blackwell et al., 2015; Kaufman, 2013). This means that some groups of students are not offered a real challenge – it is assumed that they do not have the ability and they get something simple, which you assume a person from this group can handle and succeed in. Carr and Dweck (2011) argue that this happens on the part of the teacher with the false notion that in this way students are being helped because of their "limited ability". The purpose of this on the part of the teacher has often been that the teacher wants to build the self-confidence of the student by allowing them to succeed. There is a certain danger in this, according to Dweck (1999), you may increase self-confidence temporarily and in the short term by the student answering several questions that he/she already knows, but the teacher then does not take responsibility for really developing the student's full potential.

What to consider as a teacher

Yeager and Dweck (2012) have also investigated how to influence students and their perceptions of their own abilities. For example, as a teacher, you can tell the students based on clear, scientific knowledge about the plasticity of the brain and that everyone can develop their abilities. The teacher continues with the topic of ability as developable in the form of various tasks and uses, for example, group assignments in which students work together to reflect and exemplify the dynamic in ability. Students can also write down what they have learned about ability and its potential to be developable in all people and submit for feedback. Further, a normalisation of "making mistakes" and not understanding a material or task from the very beginning is important. Classroom culture should be permeated by the exciting challenges that arise when you don't understand, when you do "wrong", and the opportunities this opens to really learn something you previously couldn't. This reduces the fear of failures in school, which take energy and worries students. In other words, it is important to teach students to deal with the failures and errors that occur during learning processes and normalise them. The purpose is to give the students tools to deal with failures and understand that incorrect answers are not proof that you do not "possess" the ability to learn, but a good opportunity to learn something you have not yet mastered.

Furthermore, the form of verbal feedback used in interaction with the student and students in classrooms is important. Boaler (2016) and Dweck (1999) have shown that it is possible as teachers to create a creative culture in the classroom through the verbal feedback that students receive. This means that you as a teacher are careful about what you praise, where the research distinguishes between feedback on the student as an individual, the student's process and the student's product (Jonsson & Beach, 2012). If you want to reinforce the student's view of ability as something that is developable and dynamic, it is important to give feedback on just this, such as "How well you have fought!" or "You didn't give up!" It is important in the use of feedback that a failure in the form of an incorrect answer or that the student gets stuck is something completely natural. As teachers, Dweck says, we need to primarily teach our students to handle situations when they don't understand right away or on the first try. We must instead emphasise the opportunity to be confronted with something you cannot, because only then you can learn something new – that you do not yet know. According to a larger review of interventions whose purpose was to develop beliefs in the malleable nature of ability (Burnette et al., 2022), small but stable effects was found in academic achievement among younger students.

Another important aspect as a teacher is to reflect on one's own view of ability. Several studies have been conducted to investigate how we view our own ability, whether it is fixed or dynamic, and how we judge and act upon other abilities from this perspective (Dweck, 1999). In other words, the research field distinguishes between theories about how to look at one's own ability and theories we have about the ability of others, which is highly relevant for active teachers who are to assess their students' abilities. Steimer and Mata (2016) investigated how adults approached changing their own abilities and at the same time whether they believed that other people had the opportunity to change their ability. The result was that the participants in the study felt that they had relatively great opportunities to develop their own abilities, but that other people's opportunities were more limited. Here it is important as a teacher to become aware of both how you look at your own ability and your beliefs and interpretations of your students' abilities.

Me and my colleague Dennis Beach (Jonsson & Beach, 2012) showed that those student teachers who had a stronger belief in a theory of ability as fixed and innate preferred to use feedback to students who emphasised the individual, for example, "How good you are!" or "How smart you are", compared to teacher students who had a view of ability as dynamic and developable. Those who preferred to see ability as dynamism preferred to a greater extent feedback that emphasised the praise of the actual process carried out by the students.

Mascret et al., (2015) conducted a study in which they examined how teachers' perceptions of ability affected their interaction with students. The results showed, among other things, that teachers of mathematics with beliefs of ability as fixed and immutable were involved in practices that rather lowered the student's motivation than strengthened it. For example, they confirmed the students' low ability by "comforting" as well as giving them simpler tasks that they could succeed in. Teachers of mathematics with a stronger belief in ability as malleable and developable, worked more to challenge students and emphasise the importance of trying.

Rattan et al., (2012) also investigated how teachers' attitudes towards ability as fixed or developable influenced their work with students. It turned out, too, that teachers with a stronger belief that ability is fixed preferred to use more feedback to comfort students for their "low ability" in mathematics. Unfortunately, by being "kind", the teacher can do students a disservice – you confirm that ability is something you have or don't have: "It doesn't matter if you're not a math person, you play football so well".

All people encounter problems in a learning process at some point where one does not understand a material or a task or have given an incorrect answer. It is important that the teacher creates a positive attitude in both the individual student and in the classroom when this situation arises. It's not a failure; it's a challenge and opportunity to learn something you can't instead of repeating what you already know. Rattan and others' (2012) results also showed that those teachers who had stronger confidence that ability is something fixed and innate to a greater extent made an initial assessment of the student and stuck to it. Those teachers who preferred a dynamic view of ability, on the other hand, held off on their assessment of students until they had more evidence for the assessment (see also Butler, 2000). These studies seek to explain that if one considers ability as something that exists/does not exist in a person, it becomes logical that assessment and grading can be carried out as soon as the teacher has formed an idea of whether the student has or does not have the ability. If you then use simple categories such as girl/boy, diagnosis/not diagnosis and so on as a basis for your assessment and generalise this information about a category to the individual student, an assessment of the student's expected ability also follows very quickly, initially, which will guide the teacher's interaction with the student. If, on the other hand, you as a teacher have an attitude towards ability as something that can be developed within the student over time, you must wait and observe over time before making an assessment. This last approach is also more in line with how the curriculum, and the school's governing documents generally state that assessment and grading should take place.

In this chapter, I have described how important it is that teachers relate to their students' perceptions of their own ability as this can affect their learning strategies, motivation, and cognitive performance. Research has shown that there are differences between individuals but that the environment in which the individual finds themselves affects how these beliefs are formed, both in the home and in the school classroom. Above all, the importance of language use is crucial. Studies show that already at the age of 4–5, children begin to form notions of ability in which they are characterised by the language of parents in the home. Then, as they continue into the world of schooling, students are influenced by the teacher's feedback. Studies show the importance of providing feedback towards the student's work process and not towards the student as a person. But also, that the teacher concretely describes ability as something dynamic for the whole class can deepen the notion in the students that they can develop and that an error is an opportunity to learn something new and not a proof that one lacks an internal, fixed ability. Finally, I address the opportunity as a teacher to reflect on one's own beliefs about ability. Whether the teacher perceives it as developable or, on the other hand, fixed and unchanging may affect the students in their classroom.

References

Blackwell, L. S., Rodriguez, S., & Guerra-Carrillo, B. (2015). Intelligence as a malleable construct. In S. Goldstein, D. Princiotta & J. A. Naglieri (Eds.), *Handbook of intelligence: Evolutionary theory, historical perspective, and current concepts* (pp. 263–282). Running Press.

Blackwell, L. S., Trzesniewski, K. H., & Dweck, C. (2007). Implicit theories of intelligence predict achievement across an adolescent transition: A longitudinal study and an intervention. *Child Development, 78*(1), 246–263.

Boaler, J. (2016). *Mathematical mindsets: Unleashing students' potential through creative math, inspiring messages and innovative teaching.* Jossey Bass Wiley.

Burnette, J. L., Knouse, L. E., Billingsley, J., Earl, S., Pollack, J. M., & Hoy, C. L. (2022). A systematic review and meta-analysis of growth mindset interventions: For whom, how, and why might such intervention work? *Psychological Bulletin, 17*(2), 1–15.

Butler, R. (2000). Making judgments about ability: The role of implicit theories of intelligence in moderating inference from temporal and social comparison information. *Journal of Personality and Social psychology, 78*(5), 965–978.

Carr, P. B., & Dweck, C. S. (2011). Intelligence and motivation. In R. J. Sternberg & S. B. Kaufman (Eds.), *The Cambridge handbook of intelligence* (pp. 748–770). Cambridge University Press.

Cury, F., Elliot, A. J., Da Fonseca, D., & Moller, A. C. (2006). The social-cognitive model of achievement motivation and the 2x2 achievement goal framework. *Journal of Personality and Social Psychology, 90,* 666–679.

De Castella, K., & Byrne, D. (2015). My intelligence may be more malleable than yours: The revised implicit theories of intelligence (self-theory) scale is a better predictor of achievement, motivation, and student disengagement. *European Journal of Psychology of Education, 30*(3), 245–267.

Dweck, C. S. (1986). Motivational processes affecting learning. *American Psychologist, 41*(10), 1040–1048.
Dweck, C. S. (1999). *Self-theories: Their role in motivation, personality, and development*. Psychology Press.
Dweck, C. S. (2012). Implicit theories. In P. Van Lange, A. Wruglanski & E. Higgins (Eds.), *Handbook of theories of social psychology* (pp. 43–62). Sage Publications Limited.
Dweck, C. S., & Legget, E. L. (1988). A social cognitive approach to motivation and personality. *Psychological Review, 95*, 256–273.
Dweck, C. S., & Master, A. (2009). Self-theories and motivation: Students' beliefs about intelligence. In K. Wentzel & A. Wigfield (Eds.), *Handbook of motivation at school* (pp. 171–195). Taylor Francis.
Dweck, C. S., & Yeager, D. S. (2019). Mindsets: A view from two eras. *Perspectives on Psychological Science, 14*(3), 481–496.
Henderlong Corpus, J., & Lepper, M. R. (2002). The effects of praise on children's intrinsic motivation: A review and synthesis. *Psychological Bulletin, 128*, 774–795.
Henderlong Corpus, J., & Lepper, M. R. (2007). The effects of person versus performance praise on children's motivation: Gender and age as moderating factors. *Educational Psychology, 27*(4), 487–508.
Jonsson, A.-C., & Beach, D. (2012). Predicting the use of praise among pre-service teachers: Influence from implicit theories of intelligence, social comparison and stereotype acceptance. *Education Inquire, 3*(2), 259–281.
Jonsson, A.-C., & Beach, D. (2017). The influence of subject disciplinary studies on students' implicit theories of intelligence and achievement goals in one Swedish upper-secondary school. *Education Inquiry, 8*(1), 50–67.
Kaufman, S. (2013). *Ungifted: Intelligence redefined*. Basic Books.
Mascret, N., Roussel, P., & Cury, F. (2015). Using implicit theories to highlight science teachers' implicit theories of intelligence. *European Journal of Psychology of Education, 30*(3), 269–280.
Middleton, M., & Midgley, C. (1997). Avoiding the demonstration of lack of ability: An underexplored aspect of goal theory. *Journal of Educational Psychology, 89*, 710–718.
Nisbett, R. (2009). *Intelligence and how to get it: Why schools and cultures count*. W.W. Norton & Company.
Patrick, H., Kaplan, A., & Ryan, A. M. (2011). Positive classroom motivational environments: Convergence between mastery goal structure and classroom social climate. *Journal of Educational Psychology, 103*(2), 367–382.
Rathel, J. M., Drasgow, E., & Christle, A. C. (2008). Effects of supervisor performance feedback on increasing preservice teachers' positive communication behaviors with students with emotional and behavioral disorders. *Journal of Emotional and Behavioral Disorders, 16*(2), 67–77.
Rattan, A., Good, C., & Dweck, C. S. (2012). "It's ok – Not everyone can be good at math": Instructors with an entity theory comfort (and demotivate) students. *Journal of Experimental Social Psychology, 48*, 731–737.
Rosenthal, R., & Jacobson, L. (1992). *Pygmalion in the classroom: Teacher expectation and pupils' intellectual development*. Irvington.
Steimer, A., & Mata, A. (2016). Motivated implicit theories of personality: My weaknesses will go away, but my strengths are here to stay. *Personality and Social Psychology, 42*, 415–429.
Yeager, D. S., & Dweck, C. S. (2012). Mindsets that promote resilience: When students believe that personal characteristics can be developed. *Educational Psychologist, 47*, 302–314.

4 An inclusive optimistic approach to inclusion

Elin Lande

In Norway there is an educational policy stating that all pupils, regardless of their physical, psychological, or social condition, have the right to be included in a class or basic group that meets their needs for social affiliation. Tistedal primary school in Halden Municipality, Norway, has come a long way in this regard. In this chapter I take a leadership perspective to discuss the process Tistedal has gone through as we have progressed towards achieving our goal of providing special education in the classroom.

The school's core concept is that teaching is to be of good quality and the pupils are to learn social skills through cooperation. The school offers positive special education through varied and flexible learning, based on evidential methods. Tistedal is an inclusive school with facilities and activities designed and physically adapted for all pupils. All pupils follow the national curriculum and belong to a specific class.

About the school

Tistedal primary school in Halden, is a year 1–7 school with two parallel classes per grade level. The school opened in 2010. There are about 300 pupils aged 6 to 12 at Tistedal, evenly distributed over the seven grade levels. Ten pupils are connected to our extended department, and about 100 of our pupils are organised in after-school activities (SFO). All 60 staff are organised in teams based on grade level.

The day-to-day leadership of Tistedal consists of the principal, the assistant principal, the head of the after-school programme (SFO), and the head of the extended department. The school accepts student teachers in a close partnership with the teacher training programme at Oestfold University College. In the autumn of 2016, Tistedal started a collaboration with the Educational and Psychological Counselling Service (PPT) in the municipalities of Halden.

Our school is referred to as an "extended school" and have a specially adapted department. This means that it is intended for multi-disabled children with different needs of support and is an integral aspect of the school. In Norway, all pupils follow the national curriculum. For a pupil to be taught in an extended department, the pupil must have physical or psychological challenges requiring their education to deviate from the curriculum in all subjects.

There are currently ten pupils in the school's extended department, and all are part of their classes with peers. Because of their disabilities they are not able to spend all day in the classroom, but they participate in classroom teaching according to their own abilities and in joint activities. As a part of our inclusive teaching, we do what we call "reverse inclusion", where we invite a few pupils at a time from the class to join the learning activities in the extended department. In this way all our pupils develop better social skills.

Background to the project

The overall aim of the project has been to reorganise special education so that all pupils can benefit from this both socially and educationally. We want all pupils at Tistedal to feel that they are part of the educational community and to develop optimally in interaction with their peers and limit their time spent alone with an adult. Tistedal was chosen because the school has an extended department, and the staff are good at positive special education and including teaching. Another reason was because repeated surveys showed that the pupils like the school (see Table 4.1) and that a high percentage of pupils were in special education programmes.

We evaluated our own teaching prior to the start of the project and reflected on how we adjusted our special education. A key question was: Can we organise our teaching in such a way that we ensure pupils' needs for social inclusion and their learning? We agreed that we had to change the traditional special needs teaching practice where the special needs teacher had pupils one to one or in small groups working on tasks that had nothing to do with the class curriculum. We wanted to change the fact that the class teacher hardly knew the pupils that require special education. We wanted all staff to know their students. We had to incorporate a common understanding when discussing both education in general and special needs education. Although not all teachers were equally positive to changing their teaching methods, everyone was willing to participate in the project. In the spring of 2017, the school's teachers completed a questionnaire as part of a halfway evaluation of the project's development work. The results showed that the staff experienced the development work in different ways. When we asked whether the reorganisation had a positive impact on the pupil social learning and the subject learning, we saw that class teachers and special education teachers were significantly more positive than subject teachers.

Table 4.1 Excerpted from the 2019 Pupil Survey (scale from 1–5)

Part year	2014–2015	2015–2016	2016–2017	2017–2018	2018–2019	2021–2022
Do you enjoy school?	4.4	4.2	4.2	4.2	4.3	4.3

Leadership situation and challenges during the project

In the spring of 2017, we evaluated the teaching at the school using the Delta model (IMTEC), which can be briefly described as an evaluation of our practice. The evaluation made it clear what we wanted to keep, what we wanted to improve, and what we wanted to eliminate. Based on these results and inspired by Robinson (2016), we made some changes within the leadership team. Hjertø (2017) emphasises that effective and learning (leadership) teams are an important factor in achieving success in development processes. Robinson's (2016) five leadership dimensions demonstrate the importance of being able to show leadership in the teachers' continued learning. As leaders, we need to actively maintain staff motivation and a continuing development of the project. We also need to ensure that our staff always have the best possible shared understanding of our goal. Another goal has been for all staff to regard their jobs as meaningful.

Earlier, Tistedal created separate lessons for pupils in need of special education. This organisation of lessons led to the reallocation of resources from other pupils and required diagnosing pupils so that sufficient resources would be allocated. This separation of teaching resulted in a reduced sense of responsibility by class teachers for pupils removed from their lessons. This is because the class teachers saw the special education teachers as having this responsibility (Robinson, 2016). This was something leadership wanted to change.

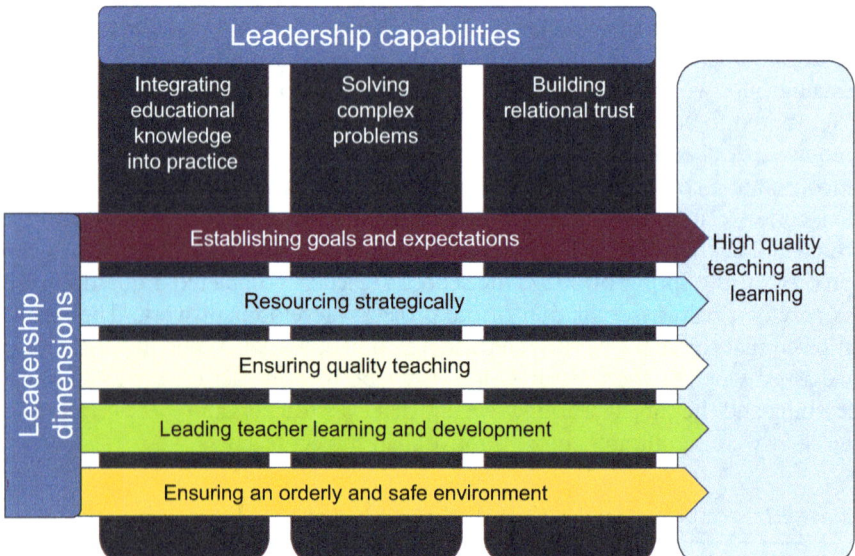

Figure 4.1 Robinson model

Source: Robinson, V.M.J., Hohepa, M., and Lloyd, C. (2009). School Leadership and Student Outcomes: Identifying what works and why. Wellington: Ministry of Education.

Additionally, organising pupils based on decisions about special educational goal, did not result in sufficient adjustment of classrooms because pupils were removed from their lessons. Because the leadership wanted more pupils to participate in ordinary lessons, it was important for the teachers to acquire the necessary skills for adjusting their classroom teaching. The leadership has now ensured that sufficient resources are available to achieve inclusion. We have clarified expectations for the project to all staff, and we have played an active role in teachers' training. Furthermore, we have regular meetings with PPT and the school owners – the municipal administration – about the project.

The organisational situation and challenges during the project

We established a working group for our development project consisting of the principal, assistant principal, special education coordinator, a coordinator who is responsible for ensuring that the pupils in grade level 1–4 who need extra reading and writing lessons receive them, the head of the extended department, and counsellors from PPT. In consultation with the leadership, the group looked for ways to achieve inclusion and what this means for the other staff. The working group is to contribute to creating understanding, acceptance, and access to adjusted teaching.

The current challenge is to share the gained experience and establish a culture of sharing so that all grade levels can work systematically on including all pupils in the classroom. We were inspired by Robinson (2016) and working according to this model. When special education is being provided in the classroom, this requires all the adults to cooperate and communicate with each other. Teachers who work towards a common goal are more unified, and they can ensure the growth and well-being of their pupils (Robinson, 2016).

It is usually more motivating to hear directly from colleagues who have been successful than to have school leaders explain it. Our goal is to establish a culture in which the staff share their experiences of mutually developing attitudes and acceptance of having all pupils in the classroom. We want to create a space for a professional teaching community in which all staff can participate in improving their skills through joint meeting places (Hargreaves & Fullan, 2014). We also hope that all staff want to contribute and feel that they can contribute.

All staff have been introduced to the meaning of adjusting teaching. All teachers have received an introduction to the theory and the different teaching strategies and have passed this on to assisting staff. The aim is that all grade levels will use Mitchell's (2014) teaching strategies to improve opportunities for learning. To achieve the best possible result for all pupils, it is important that we hold constructive grade-level-based meetings with a clarification of roles, tasks, and challenges. It is also important that staff use a common language and have a shared understanding of the strategies and why we apply them.

Educational practices and challenges during the project

As we have noted, pupils are happy at Tistedal. This has been shown in every one of the surveys from the last six years. We must continue our efforts to maintain these good results. The satisfaction level, however, falls when asked if they can work in peace and quietness during lessons. This may indicate that it is not enough structure, and that routines are lacking in the classroom. We need to improve this. The grade levels already systematically apply to the teaching strategies point to increased pupil participation and increased pressure to learn and to share their learning during the lessons.

In conversations with pupils, they describe the lessons as more varied than before, and they must work on their own thoughts. They also seem to like the unity in the classroom and to make new friends. The pupils also say that they have got to know the adults better because more adults are now in the classroom. Another goal is for all pupils to experience varied teaching, that improves their motivation. This makes sharing the positive experiences of both pupils and adults with other staff important.

Before this project, special education was mainly organised into different small groups in each grade level. However, not everyone had the same special educational needs. The special education teachers "took their own path" in the groups, that is, the content was loosely taken from the grade level's goals. The school became aware of the fact that pupils removed from the classroom for several lessons a week were missing a lot of learning. We also observed that some teachers lacked confidence in their ability to teach students with intellectual disabilities, that is, low self-efficacy in their teaching. A detailed discussion of the causes and consequences of self-efficacy, will be further developed in the chapter by Monica Reichenberg (2024).

All teachers providing special education lessons were qualified special education teachers. Over the last five years, the school has assigned a full-time position for intensive learning, which has been at importance in implementing this project. It is intended as a short-term, goal-oriented initiative from the school in reading, writing or arithmetic in grade levels 1–4. The aim is to provide early support and follow-up for preventive issues for pupils in need.

Three years into this project, we saw a change. The reorganisation of special education has led to a greater subject and social sharing among all pupils.

- Pupils achieving slightly better results in national tests and other survey materials.
- Pupils feeling that the teaching strategies are more visible in the classroom.
- Pupils experiencing a more inclusive learning environment.
- Pupils expressing that they receive more support and help from the adults.
- Pupils expressing that it is easier to learn together with the other pupils in the classroom.

And even the staff experienced changes:

- Staff work is followed up more closely by leadership.
- Staff have a safer and better working environment.

- Staff take a more collective responsibility for each other's teaching.
- Staff feel that it is useful to share experiences with each other.
- Staff understand each other better when they talk about the challenges facing pupils.
- Staff take more collective responsibility for pupil learning.
- Staff take greater responsibility for pupil inclusion.
- Staff have greater acceptance for differences among pupils and meet them in different ways.

New methods that have been implemented

The project also experienced the resistance that often occurs when change is expected. The special education teachers and assistants were the biggest opponents. They were also the ones who experienced the biggest changes through our reorganisation. After several years of intense pressure in various projects and development work at the schools in Halden, there has been some frustration among the teacher staff. Previous projects have not always been properly followed up, and this has resulted in some resistance to change among the staff.

The leadership has endeavoured to inform and involve staff from the start. The school has benefitted from this process, and it has been a great help in achieving what we wanted to achieve. The development work strives to make the school a professional educational community (Stollar, 2014).

The parent group was initially sceptical about this project. Several parents with children eligible for special education were afraid that their children would lose the entitlement. We have listened attentively to the parents' questions, reassuring them and informing them thoroughly throughout the project. To make sure that the pupils really benefit, we interviewed the pupils receiving special education in spring 2017. The pupils' responses were very positive. Students say that they have learnt more, have made more friends, and feel better about school. The parent group is now positive because they have seen the positive effects of the project.

The staff have attended several information meetings, courses, and lectures linked to inclusion. Course content has consisted of review of the theory and practical testing of different teaching strategies. Robinson (2016) emphasises how the importance of the indirect influence and attitudes from the leadership, through the teachers, is passed on to the pupils. Two important prerequisites for leading the teachers' training and development are good relationships among the leadership and the staff and a safe social climate. In addition, Robinson emphasises the importance of the leadership's motivation and commitment in training and development of teachers. This means that the leadership is not only active in staff meetings and development work but also in more informal activities. In this way, we can make staff feel appreciated. School leaders oversee all teaching staff, but relations with individuals are also of great importance. Teachers will also continue to keep and develop their independence in a professional educational community.

We spent the first part of the process surveying the organisation (Skandsen et al., 2014). In the spring of 2018, we conducted an evaluation meeting with all the staff. The staff were encouraged to highlight what they wanted to preserve, remove, or improve. After that, each staff member was asked to complete a form and compile their results with the results of colleagues within the same subject. The compiled results were then presented to the rest of the staff.

Current practice

Six years into this project, we see a significant change in teaching methods. At the beginning of the project, we looked for teaching methods that made better use of our adult resources. Beginning with *station work*, using groups where the pupils move from one group to another throughout the lesson, as a method, we saw that we could divide the class into smaller groups. All stations have different activities, and pupils are allowed to work on different tasks during the lesson. In our experience, it is easier to adjust teaching of individual pupils in a small group, and adults get to know the pupils better. Olivia Carter (2024) elaborated further in her chapter about the importance of adjusted/differentiated teaching for the best possible learning for the students.

We use the station method for a few lessons per week in each grade level. To achieve the best results using the station method, we have increased the staff during these lessons. Two classes share both class teachers, an assistant, and a special education teacher which all take part in the lesson.

Mitchell (2014) describes 27 strategies in his book *What Really Works in Special and Inclusive Education*. We have chosen to focus on six of them. We have worked with *cooperative learning*, where pupils learn from each other, *collaborative learning*, where pupils work together in groups; *social skills*, where pupils learn positive interaction with other; *cognitive strategies*, where pupils learn through being aware of one's own learning, learn different ways of thinking strategically; *memorisation strategies*, where pupils learn how to remember more; and *inclusive teaching*, where we adjust the teaching to all pupils. Matt Maquire (2024) describes a practical example and develop further how students use their problem-solving skills as a group in his chapter and the ability to be aware of one's own learning is also discussed and further developed in the chapter by Ann-Katrin Swärd (2024).

Through systematic testing and evaluation during the project, all the staff have had the opportunity to test the strategies in their classrooms. The strategies were tested in subjects that the class would have taken according to the subject curriculum and adjusted for the different pupils. We now see that pupils are also implementing these strategies. Both pupils and staff now accept that all pupils belong in the same classroom. All teachers have changed their practices and become better at adjusting their teaching. The assistants are no longer the pupils' personal assistants but are part of the classroom environment and know all the pupils.

An inclusive optimistic approach to inclusion 39

Figure 4.2 Cooperative learning and station work: The blond boy is teaching a group of peers about dinosaurs

A glimpse of everyday life

During a day at school, we can see that first-grade pupils are collecting letters. The letters adorn the walls of the classroom and the corridors. Pupils are walking around, collecting the letters and form as many words as they can with the letters. The teacher helps pupils report the number of words, and together they check whether the pupils have spelled the words correctly.

Outside grade level two is having art and crafts lesson. They work in groups and have been given the task of creating a human body using "land art". To create it, the pupils need to search the playground for leaves, sticks, stones, and other things they can use. Then they try to cooperate on how to make the body. The teacher walks around, coaching the pupils, questions are adjusted to the pupils' abilities.

Grade level 3 is doing station work. Two classes, 42 pupils, are divided into five groups. The stations are placed in two classrooms and in a smaller room. There are two teachers, two assistants, and one special needs teacher this lesson. Each group starts at a different station. One station practise reading and read texts in different ways. The pupils are reading in pairs and as a group, together with an assistant.

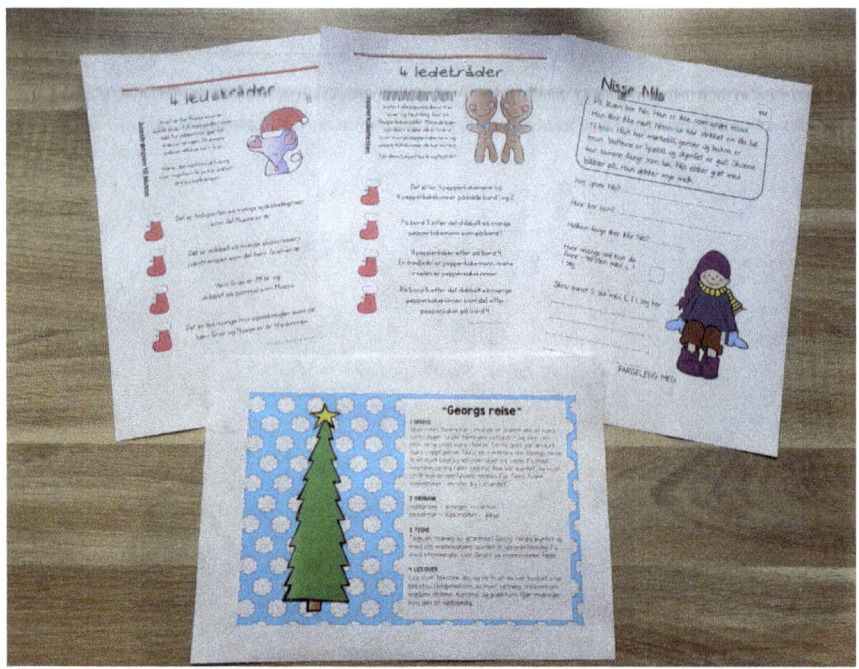

Figure 4.3 Text samples, different levels

One station has writing exercises encouraging the pupils to write their own books, using "story starters", and pupils are to finish the story based on the first sentence and the picture. Before they start writing, they talk to the teacher about their different ideas. The special education teacher then helps those who need help.

One station has reading comprehension where pupils receive different texts and a picture, and the text explains how to colour the picture.

At one station, pupils play Scrabble with help from an assistant. The last station works with word classes. The pupils are divided into 2 teams. The task is done as a relay race.

One pupil from each team runs up to the teacher, who gives them a word. The pupil then runs back to his team and places the word in the right place in the form, listing the word classes. All team members feel that they can handle the task, and the team experiences a sense of cohesion.

In grade level 4, pupils are working on mathematics. They use computers and software that comes with the textbook. The pupils work on multiplication, and the software adjusts the tasks to the pupils. If a pupil is struggling with one multiplication table, they will be given a simpler task. Pupils who master the large multiplication table receive increasingly difficult tasks.

Grade level 5 work on the topic of municipalities in Norway, and all pupils are creating tourism advertisements for different municipalities. Pupils need to look for information online and complete the template. The teacher assesses

An inclusive optimistic approach to inclusion 41

Figure 4.4 Story starters samples

Figure 4.5 Read and colour samples

42 *Positive Special Education*

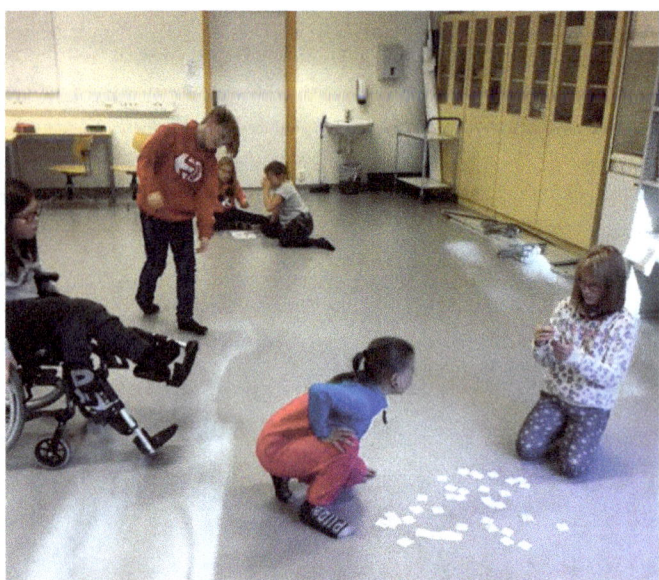

Figure 4.6 Word class relay race

both the content and the layout of the advertising. Everything looks the same to the pupils, but the content varies because the pupils find different information. The teacher adjusts the task so that some pupils can find a lot of information about their municipalities, while others get easier tasks. Everything is written down using a computer.

Grade level 6 has home economics class. They are making cinnamon rolls. Two pupils who receive special education in mathematics have received the recipe in advance. They have calculated the quantities of all the ingredients they need. They also have calculated the cost of the ingredients, visited the store with the special education teacher, and purchased what they need. Pupils are responsible for paying with the correct amount of money. The class is divided into groups, and each pupil is responsible for their task. Someone measures out the ingredients, another stirs them in the bowl, others do dishes, and one sets the table.

Grade level 7 is doing the weekly test. Questions from the whole week's lessons in different subjects are hanging from trees in the playground. The pupils run in pairs to a question, read the question, and run to the teacher and tell her the answer. This method allows pupils to collaborate, be active, and demonstrate to the teacher what they learned during the past week. A pupil who does not know the answer will be assisted by their running companion, and if neither can find the answer, they will be assisted to find the answer by the teacher. This activity follows the new and updated national curriculum from 2020 about public health and life-mastering and aim to introduce our pupils to the joys of physical activity.

Our conclusion

Tistedal primary school has seen a significant change in our teaching. Previously, the school was a traditional Norwegian school in which special education took place in separate rooms behind closed doors. Pupils receiving special education had little social contact with the pupils in the open classroom. Today, in our school the pupils believe they learn more, have more friends, there is less bullying, and there is a greater acceptance of each other's differences. We have a school where teachers use positive special education in every lesson. Our pupils help each other and are aware that all pupils have their own special talents. There are, of course, matters that still need to be improved, but both groups of pupils, those who worked well previously and those who were taken out of the classroom, now feel that they enjoy school more. We see a slight improvement in their results in academic subjects, but the social and mental benefits for all students are even more important. As our former principal said: "We will never return to our previous teaching methods, and we will continue to use adjusted teaching and special education methods in the open classroom!"

References

Carter, O. (2024). Differentiated teaching. In M. Reichenberg, A.-K. Swärd & C. Shipton (Eds.), *Positive special education: Theories, application and inspiration*. Routledge.

Fullan, M., & Hargreaves, A. (2014). *Arbeidskultur for bedre læring i alle skoler. Hva er nødvendig lærerkapital?*. Kommuneforlaget.

Hjertø, K. B. (2017). Rektor som teameier: Kapasistetsbygging gjennom teamarbeid i. In M. Aas & Paulsen J. M. (Red.), *Ledelse i fremtidens skole*. Fagbokforlaget.

IMTEC. https://imtec.no

Maguire, M. (2024). Teaching functional literacy to pupils with SEN. In M. Reichenberg, A.-K. Swärd & C. Shipton (Eds.), *Positive special education: Theories, applications and inspiration* (pp. 70–76). Routledge.

Mitchell, D. (2014). *Hvad der virker i inkluderende undervisning - evidensbaserte undervisningsstrategier*. Dalfolo.

Reichenberg, M. (2024). Positive special education: Why are teachers' and students' self-efficacy important? Consequences for reading instruction and civic education. In M. Reichenberg, A.-K. Swärd & C. Shipton (Eds.), *Positive special education: Theories, applications and inspiration* (pp. 7–22). Routledge.

Robinson, V.M.J., Hohepa, M., and Lloyd, C. (2009). *School Leadership and Student Outcomes: Identifying what works and why*. Wellington: Ministry of Education.

Skandsen, T., Wærnes, J. I., & Lindvig, L. (2014). *Entusiasme for endring. En håndbok for skoleledere*. Gyldendal Akademisk.

Stollar, L. J. (2014). *Teachers' perception of a professional learning community model and its impact on teaching and learning*. Widener University.

Swärd, A.-K. (2024). Positive special education: Challenge students to read and write in a creative way without fixed material. In M. Reichenberg, A.-K. Swärd & C. Shipton (Eds.), *Positive special education: Theories, applications and inspiration* (pp. 95–103). Routledge.

5 Inviting students to develop their capabilities through narrative

Ian Bearcroft

This chapter will discuss some key questions in special educational practice, with reference to teaching literacy to children with special educational needs in special schools in England. It will describe the authors context and Archdale School where he teaches and the principles and possibilities of teaching literacy visually, using a multisensory approach. It will discuss how one might think about planning for learning, delivering learning, and will conclude by pulling these strands together into an example lesion at the end.

Archdale School

Archdale School is a state-maintained primary school located in Sheffield, in the north of England. It is a special school with 95 students. The school is located the south of the city and has a very diverse community.

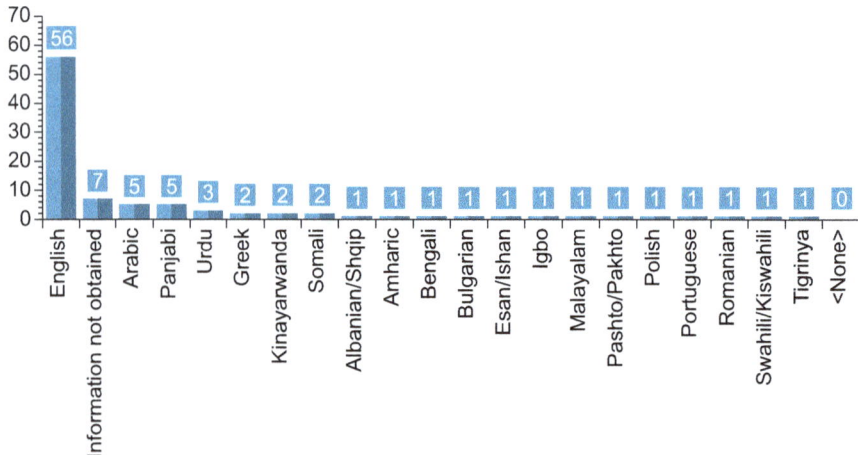

Figure 5.1 First languages spoken by students at Archdale School
Source: Archdale School 2024.

DOI: 10.4324/9781003509141-5

Inviting students to develop capabilities through narrative 45

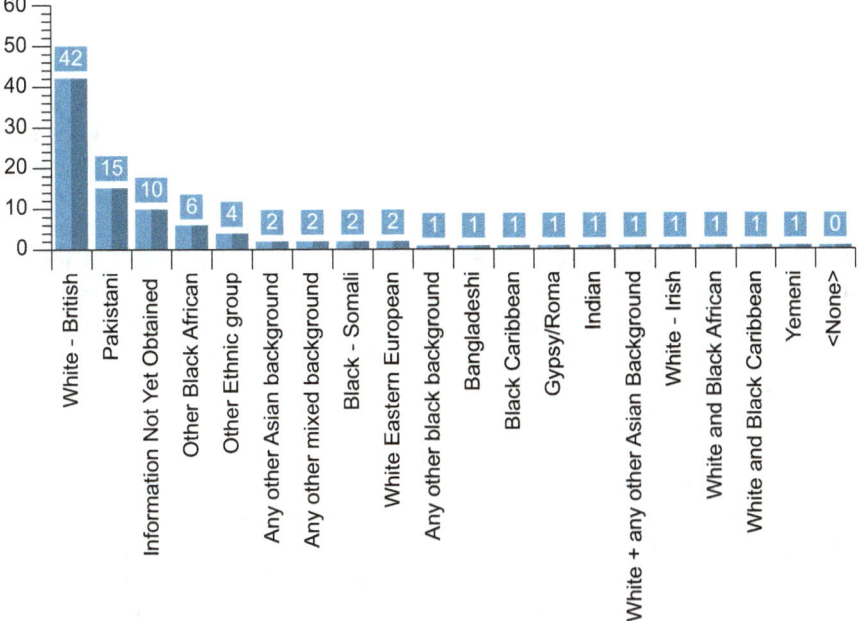

Figure 5.2 Student ethnicities present at Archdale School
Source: Archdale School 2024.

Parental involvement at Archdale School

Parental involvement in the school takes the form of parents' evenings, daily communication books, the parent teacher association. Parents are encouraged to become school governors, if this is a responsibility they would welcome. Classroom teachers like me aim to meet the diverse needs and preferences of our children's families. Some families want more contact and involvement than others, and some want different things at different times. In some cases, I will set targets and learning outcomes for work across both home and school settings with that work being a collaboration between families and school; however some families are content to let schoolwork be for school and home life be for home. I work in a setting in which I am privileged with a great deal of freedom to meet the needs of my students and their families on an individual basis.

What is inclusion?

Inclusion of students with special educational needs within educational settings has been a feature of educational policy in the UK for over 40 years (Warnock, 1978; Children and Families Act, 2014), and the UK

Government remain committed to the inclusive education of disabled children to this day (Department for Education & Department of Health, 2015, p. 25). Unlike mainstream schools, all children in English special schools have an Education and Health Care Plan (EHCP), which sets out the areas of need and provision for a child and is reviewed annually for the lifespan of the document (Children and Families Act, 2014). An EHCP contains the overarching goals which teachers break down in their termly learning intentions for each learner, regardless of subject. This breakdown document has many names, depending on the school concerned (Department for Education, 2021, 2022). English special schools are overwhelmingly organised into progression frameworks which broadly correspond to the four subcategories of intellectual disability listed in the ICD-11 (World Health Organization, 2019).

My own class has nine students, four of which are accessing a semi-formal and five accessing an informal curriculum. Both sets of learners have individualised learning plans based on their Education and Healthcare Plans, and it is my task as the class teacher to express these core targets within the context of subjects such as communication, physical activity, or mathematics, whilst coordinating specialist support from external professionals and stakeholders, including families and the students themselves who may have very specific interests about the learning and the learning environment. This is, in my view, a recipe for positive educational experience for informal and semi-formal learners.

How are we to think about our learning intentions?

The tendency in special education practice is towards learning that is bespoke to each learner. Once we know what our learners' key learning intentions are, we may turn ourselves to the task of finding an apt mechanism to facilitate these. Alongside the supporting documents and progression frameworks that accompany a school curriculum pathway (Archdale School, 2023), teachers are supported in their practice by evidence-based frameworks in the delivery of education to young people with learning disabilities and differences. SCERTS, for example, is a framework used widely in the United States and the UK, designed to support learners on the autism spectrum targeting social communication (SC) emotional regulation (ER) through the use of transactional supports (TS) and can be used in a number of ways, including designing developmentally appropriate learning supports and educational planning. It is a useful joint framework to support joint target writing with external professionals like speech and language therapists.

However one coordinates the learning intentions, once the core learning for a term is established, these intentions can be worked on through a multiplicity of contexts or subjects. This workflow ensures bespoke and individualised provision into the fabric of the planning cycle. Inclusive practice in special schools in England often refers to the practice of meeting a diverse set of learning needs in each lesson. Because of this, teachers in special schools have a great deal of autonomy to meet the needs of each individual learner, drawing on and triangulating information from a broad set of sources. Core learning unique to the individual are generally combined with subject specific learning such that a key communication strategy, the use of a core vocabulary board, for example, may be included within a literacy lesion in the morning and a food technology session in the afternoon. In this way the core learning can remain ongoing in a wide variety of settings to support generalising these skills.

The core learning as expressed in a student's Education and Healthcare Plan has dominance over the subject knowledge of a particular session and has an aims-based approach (Reiss & White, 2013), rather than a pedagogy based on the acquisition of subject knowledge alone. In a primary setting such as Archdale School, classroom teachers are responsible for the process of setting core and subject targets for the students in their classes. In a secondary or college setting, children may transition between classes for sessions with subject specialists. In secondary or college settings, subject specialists must likewise refer to the core learning intentions expressed in individual learners' Education and Healthcare Plans in their subject-specific planning. Teachers in secondary or college settings thus work with the individual students' tutor group teachers who set the core learning. This is a highly collaborative process and requires school leaders to provide robust organisational infrastructure to support it.

Readers learn best within a community of readers, where an awareness of literacy is given priority and celebrated. This environment may require a multisensory approach using visual, tactile, and auditory experiences to promote the engagement of all learners. A communication-rich environment should be established and tailored to support the needs of each learner with opportunities for wide and exciting literary experiences (Dockrell et al., 2012). Teaching stories and narratives can be enhanced across all curriculum pathways by using a multisensory approach such as story sacks (National Literacy Trust, 2022) to support reading from the outset. Regardless of curriculum pathway, home-school involvement will have a positive impact, with learners taking home some form of literary experience to share and bring back to school. Some students may benefit from augmented and alternative communication systems to support expressive language, and blending the sounds required for learning through phonics (American Speech Language Hearing Association, 2023) may be used in collaboration with a school's speech and language therapist and communication team. Schools should take a systematic approach when reviewing the effective practice of teaching and adapting phonics at regular intervals.

For learners on a semi-formal curriculum pathway and developmentally before formal Phonics, research has shown that encouraging learners to become storytellers using personal experiences or through approaches like Lis'nTell (Coigley, 2021), which approach communication development in a student-centred way that provides a positive way into literacy for learners. Stories may be supported with developmentally appropriate language supports which scaffold and break down sentences using symbols (Frome Loeb, 2001) and colour coded to indicate subjects, verbs, objects, and modifiers, or use of core vocabulary boards. Language supports of this kind contain word sets based on the pronouns, verbs, prepositions, and demonstratives, which make up to 89% of a pre-schooler's vocabulary (Fallon et al., 2001) together with the fringe words that are specific to the situation or session being taught.

For learners on an informal curriculum pathway, joint attention may be the goal. Literacy may be supported at this level through the use of tactile resources, drama, and combining verbal and non-verbal techniques such as gesture, rhythm, and rhyme can intensify meaning through repetition. Communicative approaches such as intensive interaction (Nind & Hewett, 2005) and the use of voice output communication aids and responds to gestures and vocalisations, which may be useful ways to respond positively and interactively to children's contributions to narratives when using an approach like Lis'nTell.

Making learning irresistible

Regardless of curriculum pathway, developments in primary school education in England over the last ten years have moved away from checklists based on typically developing children and towards encouraging active participation and engagement (Rochford, 2016). It is no longer enough to have our learners with special educational needs to attend physically in the space; we require them to actively engage in their learning. Attention Autism is an approach aimed at practical delivery of lessons developed by Gina Davies. Attention Autism provides a set of strategies with a progression framework that can be used by school staff to build the communication, interaction, and attentional skills of children with intellectual disabilities (Watson et al., 2017). The key principle of Attention Autism is that children are offered an irresistible invitation to learn by using highly motivating and engaging activities, which are worth paying attention to and communicating about. This allows the child to opt in spontaneously, rather than being forced to communicate or attend. Pragmatically, this means if a child gets up or is not interested in the lesson, it falls on us as educators to be motivating enough to make the activity irresistible. For those learners who are beginning to regulate themselves with less support, the zones of regulation programme (Kuypers, 2011) has been designed to help young people self-identify when their arousal levels are too high or low and offer a strategy to help the young person stay in an optimal state of arousal, for example, jogging on the spot when arousal is low or taking deep breaths if arousal is too high.

This is by no means an exhaustive list; the author merely invites the reader to turn the conventional view of the curriculum on its head. Typically, mainstream curricula are arranged by subjects with their accompanying discrete and specific knowledge (Reiss & White, 2013). However, our more complex learners increasingly require that we treat subjects as the mechanism through which deep learning of core learning from a student's EHCP is achieved. A positive approach to pedagogy also requires educators to plan for learning in a way that is bespoke to each learner within a class. As a general principle, it should be born in mind that while mainstream learners can generally adapt to the needs of the curriculum, our more complex learners cannot (Male, 2015, pp.10–11).

Setting up the environment for learning

If we are looking for genuine engagement from our learners, it follows that we must make learning irresistible for our learners. We may be assisted in this endeavour through the careful preparation and control of the learning environment. For children on a formal curriculum pathway, individual timetables and written schedules may be used to help them navigate into a session. For those on a semi-formal or informal curriculum pathway, a symbol-based equivalent or object of reference may likewise support transitions. Routines such as dimming the lights, cue music, and other routines like "tidy up time" may likewise support children's understanding as it gives focus to the lesson content. A high level of personal organisation is recommended with everything necessary for the delivery of the session being ready to hand and prepared well in advance.

In addition to student-specific communication supports required to access a session, overall, in-task visual supports are helpful to assist children to predict the purpose and sequence of a session – for students on formal curriculum pathways, written schedules may be used, and symbol based or drawn schedules may be used for learners on semi-formal and informal curriculum pathways. It should be noted that control of the environment does not imply that all control is in the hands of the teacher, however (Lacey, 1991), and it may be necessary to consider classroom arrangements which include areas for specific sensory regulation or access to emotionally regulating objects and activities for students who need them (Prizant et al., 2006, pp. 121–123).

Putting it all together in a sample lesson plan from my class at Archdale School – *Pete The Cat I love my white shoes (Litwen, 2014).*

Class: Fox	Curriculum area: My Communication (semi-formal and informal curriculum pathway)
Rationale Fox class consists of ten primary aged learners across the whole of key stage 1 and 2. Fox class contains learners on both informal and semi-formal curriculum pathways and have thus been grouped based on complexity of learning needs, rather than their progress within key stage 1 or 2. Fox class will be split into 3 subgroups to maximise children's ability to attend to the session as well as providing learning extensions and regulation time before or after learning, as required. These subgroups will operate as a carousel of learning and consist of three posts with a key learning post, a post with extension activities, and a post with free play for emotional regulation. Tiering by ability has been unsuccessful in previous attempts to teach this session, so groupings will be determined in the moment based on individual learners' state of emotional regulation. This should appropriate distribution based on need and readiness to learn. Fox class contains a large population of learners who drop to the floor during transitions if they are anxious, bespoke, developmentally appropriate transactional supports will be used to make transitions. These supports have been designed following a SCEETS assessment to determine developmental stage and the appropriate range of supports. This is true of both supports used universally to transition, as well as the in-task visual supports (i.e., core bards, switched, etc.) If learners are unable to transition, whole session alternatives may be accessed as per list. If students want to spend more time in one of the posts, this is possible – judgement is required for this, and class reflections will pick up and discuss the thought process required by staff supporting children to facilitate them to make increasing better decisions when supporting the children.	**Organisation and deployment of support staff** Post 1: key story post – teacher plus 1 support staff I will make the learning irresistible by selecting the text and designing the props which support it, with my students' special interests in mind. This ensures a multisensory approach which is tailored to the eccentricities of my learners. The text uses repetition, which lends itself to a Lis'nTell approach; know the special interests of the kids – music, Lis'n tell guitar Props per kid Visuals per kid Post 2 extension tasks Second post will have extensions tasks for the formal learners – symbol matching for the semi, exploratory sensory for the informal – linked to individual EHCP goals Post 3 play post with emotionally regulating activities for the children

Inviting students to develop capabilities through narrative 51

Learning Objectives (WALT: We are learning to)			
To actively participate in a session (semi-circle of chairs so children can cut out is required)			
To share time with other learners			
To use language supports expressively to participate To jointly attend to staff modelling the use of developmentally appropriate language supports			
Expressive communication Button GG AAM AO LB Core board GG			
Modelling language supports Buttons Z, OG Core boards DO, AB, EA, MJ, EA.			
Core vocab	Fringe vocab	Resources	Interventions for particular needs
More, finished, turn, my	Shoe, Red, Blue, Brown, White, Oh no!	Talking cell, core vocabulary board	Supporting children who struggle to transition by giving time, key symbol or object of reference, or a motivating item where necessary
Assessment:		Evaluation of the children's learning and my practice:	

Conclusion

This chapter has discussed a broad range of concepts which may be applied to achieve a positive approach across all areas of the curriculum. It has challenged conventional notions of learning environment and where learning can be said to take place, focusing on the teaching of literacy from a predominantly English perspective. It has outlined and highlighted the need to make learning, and the supports which facilitate learning, bespoke to each individual learner within a class and discussed planning with both core learning intentions as well as subject specific learning intentions in mind. It has proposed a model of the curriculum which supports teachers in the task of triangulating through consultation with a multidisciplinary team of professionals, including families in order to devise developmentally appropriate learning intentions which address the specific learning requirements of each learner. It has argued for a particular vision of inclusion and inclusive practice which has a support base in the literature, in order to have the most positive outcomes for children in special education.

References

American Speech Language Hearing Association. (2023). *Augmentative and alternative communication* [online]. Retrieved January 17, 2023, from https://www.asha.org/public/speech/disorders/aac/

Archdale School. (2023). *Our curriculum* [online]. https://www.archdale.sheffield.sch.uk/teaching-and-learning/new-curriculum

Children and Families Act. (2014). Retrieved August 22, 2024, from https://www.legislation.gov.uk/ukpga/2014/6/contents

Coigley, L. (2021). Lis'n Tell: Live inclusive storytelling. In N. Grove (Ed.), *Storytelling, special needs and disabilities* (2nd ed., pp. 45–52). Routledge.

Department for Education. (2021). *Education, health and care plans – reporting year 2021* [online]. https://explore-education-statistics.service.gov.uk/find-statistics/education-health-and-care-plans/2021

Department for Education. (2022). *Special educational needs and disability: An analysis and summary of data sources* [online]. https://assets.publishing.service.gov.uk/government/uploads/system/uploads/attachment_data/file/1082518/Special_educational_needs_publication_June_2022.pdf

Department for Health; Department for Education. (2015). *Special educational needs and disability code of practice: 0 to 25 years. Statutory guidance for organisations which work with and support children and young people who have special educational needs or disabilities* [online]. https://assets.publishing.service.gov.uk/government/uploads/system/uploads/attachment_data/file/398815/SEND_Code_of_Practice_January_2015.pdf

Dockrell, J. E., Bakopoulou, I., Law, J., Spencer, S., & Lindsay, G. (2012). *Developing a communication supporting classrooms observation tool* [online]. Department of Education. https://assets.publishing.service.gov.uk/government/uploads/system/uploads/attachment_data/file/219634/DFE-RR247-BCRP8.pdf

Fallon, K. A., Light, J. C., Kramer Paige, T. (2001). Enhancing vocabulary selection for preschoolers who require augmentative and alternative communication (AAC). *American Journal of Speech-Language Pathology, 10*(1), 81–94.

Frome Loeb, D. (2001). Case studies on the efficacy of expansions and subject-verb-object models in early language intervention. *Child Language Teaching and Therapy, 17*(1), 35–53.

Kuypers, L. (2011). *The Zones of regulation*. Social Thinking Publishing.

Lacey, P. (1991). Managing the classroom environment. In C. Tilstone (Ed.), *Teaching pupils with severe learning difficulties*. David Fulton.

Litwen, E. (2014). *Pete the Cat I love my white shoes*. Harper Collins.

Male, D. (2015). Learners with SLD and PMLD: Provision, policy and practice. In P. Lacey, R. Ashdown, P. Jones, H. Lawson & M. Pipe (Eds.) *The Routledge companion to severe, profound and multiple learning difficulties* (pp.9–18). Routledge.

National Literacy Trust. (2022). *How to make and use a story sack* [online]. https://literacytrust.org.uk/resources/how-make-and-use-story-sack/

Nind, M., & Hewett, D. (2005). *Access to communication: Developing the basics of communication with people with severe learning difficulties through intensive interaction*. David Fulton Publishers.

Prizant, B. M., Wetherby, A. M., Rubin, E., Laurent, A. C., & Rydell, P. J. (2006). *The SCERTS model: A comprehensive educational approach for children with autism spectrum disorders*. Paul H. Brookes Publishing.

Reiss, M. J., & White, J. (2013). *An Aims-based curriculum: The significance of human flourishing for schools.* Institute of Education Press.
Rochford, D. (2016). *The Rochford review: Final report – Review of assessment for pupils working below the standard of national curriculum tests.* Department for Education.
Warnock, H. M. (1978). *Report of the committee of enquiry into the education of handicapped children and young people.* Her Majesty's Stationery Office.
Watson, J., Davies, G., Winterton, A. (2017). An evaluation of the attention autism approach with young children with autism. *Good Autism Practice, 18*(2), 79–93.
World Health Organization. (2019). *International classification of diseases for mortality and morbidity statistics (11th revision).* Retrieved from https://icd.who.int/

6 Digital tools in the classroom

Ann Johansson and Alexandra Kappel

When it comes to finding different ways to develop pupil's abilities in relation to syllabi, teaching pupils with an intellectual disability can be challenging. For example, how can we develop these pupils' writing skills when they have not yet really learned how to read or write? Like Swärd (2024), we believe that pupils learn better when linguistic activities are fun and that it is important for teachers to use imagination in creating activities. The question is how we might capture this in our teaching so that we can create a sense of coherence (Antonovsky, 2014), where the teaching becomes manageable, comprehensible, and meaningful for the pupils. Using digital tools is one way, and we vary our teaching with them. It does not matter if it sometimes gets a little wrong because that is when we – both pupils and teachers – learn something new.

When teaching with digital tools, it is important that work take place in dialogue with the pupils. Leaving pupils to work with assignments alone may result in the pupils testing their way to find the correct answer instead of working on developing their abilities. Digital tools can also contribute to more physical movement and can document things that pupils can return to. When it comes to assessment, digital tools provide opportunities for co-assessment between colleagues and observation of knowledge development.

Digital tools as a pedagogical tool

Positive special education is the starting point in our teaching, and we work variedly, and digital tools are part of this. Should pupils practise creating readable handwriting, or should they practise writing a text? The one does not eliminate the other, but if the pupils are going to practise their handwriting, they should practise with a pencil. When writing a text, we try to vary the writing with a pencil and a digital tool. In our teaching, we use different digital writing tools based on the pupils' different needs.

When pupils write texts, the support of speech synthesis may be needed. It helps pupils spell but also hear if they have written what they intended to write. It can be difficult in the beginning since many pupils want to revise their writing directly, but we first practise expressing ourselves in text and then

DOI: 10.4324/9781003509141-6

revising the text afterward. For those who need additional support in their writing process, we use digital writing tools that provide image support when text is written. Speech synthesis is also functional when it comes to verbal presentations, as pupils can listen to the text that has been written. This makes it easier for pupils who cannot read yet but who in this way can "read" and practise their text and thus take a step towards becoming more independent. Yet another aspect when it comes to teaching with digital tools is pupils using the same assignment as the rest of the class.

We work with developing pupils' mindset so it can become more of a growth mindset rather than a fixed one (Dweck, 2017). That is, we praise the efforts in pupils' work instead of the result. Pupils must know it is worth the struggle, that they should not give up, and that digital tools are an aid in their schoolwork.

Digital narratives

A digital narrative is a method that Ohler (2013) finds useful in developing pupils' literacy. The text still has a central role in the working process, but other forms of expression are also important, for example, sound and images. According to Andersson (2014), pupils develop and are stimulated when they get to use different media in expressing and communicating a message that becomes more than just a text.

We started working with digital narratives in our teaching, and we often work with interdisciplinarity, that is, we work with the same theme in different subjects at the same time. We combined this work with learning about the human body in the subject of Swedish, science, as well as the subject of art. The connecting link became a digital tool to make a short film. We started to work with what a human body looks like, and after that, the pupils made a character out of salt dough. Then, they began to write a story about the character, and this text functioned as a kind of script for the short film. When they were done with everything, we discussed together how they should move the character and props so it turns out as they had written in their story. Then, they worked in pairs, making the short film by moving the character and props little by little and photographing them one shot at a time. The pupils were super satisfied with their short films, and from simple means, they created professional films. When one of the pupils was finished and watched the result of the movie, the pupil expressed that it was the best day at school.

The *Early Learning and Educational Technology Policy Brief* (2016) describes how important it is to let pupils use pictures when they write a text – they start from the picture and develop the text from it. Shipton (2024) has similar experiences when she uses a movie to develop her pupils' writing skills. Our experiences tell us that when a creative process is involved in pupils' writing process, it is easier for them to write a text.

In our experience, digital tools are incredibly motivating for pupils to work with. As soon as they knew that the goal of the writing was to make a short film, their motivation was raised considerably, and the pupils had an easier time struggling through eventual difficulties in the assignments. Developing pupils' self-efficacy in their ability to perform in school, as well as outside school, is important (Reichenberg, 2024). The more self-efficacy they have, the more likely they are to try, endure difficulties, and perform better.

Verbal presentation through an avatar

We practise verbal presentations in different ways towards the end goal – doing a presentation in front of the classmates. Pupils also get to work with presentations about something they worked with in a subject (i.e., science subjects, social study subjects) with the help of an avatar. Wood et al., (1976) state that interaction support, "scaffolding", is important for the development of different abilities. The teacher needs to be perceptive and flexible, and the goal is that the support shall gradually decrease so that pupils develop independence.

When we worked with the theme "The fantastic human", the younger pupils got the assignment to create an avatar that should speak English. In the subject of science, we worked with space and discussed if there was life in space other than human beings. From this discussion, the pupils got an assignment in the subject of art to imagine and draw a picture of an alien. This would then become a living avatar with the help of a learning tablet and an app. The pupils also recorded their presentation and added it to the app. We learned English words that were connected to space, and the pupils introduced their alien in English to their classmates. The pupils worked on things they were not very comfortable with, but the digital tools created such motivation that they were willing to challenge themselves. We also experienced that it was easier for the pupils to work with the assignment when the focus was not on the pupil as a person but instead on the avatar.

Interactive stories

When we work with different digital tools (learning tablet and apps), we can see a clear development in a pupil's learning curve. The more access they have to digital technology, the more they develop, which Andersson (2014) also believes in when she describes how pupils develop literacy when they get access to different media. When it comes to pupils' writing development, many of our pupils find it difficult to produce longer texts – above all for our older pupils, where the knowledge requirements in the subject of Swedish increased compared to our younger children. In order to challenge and develop our pupils, we started using a digital tool online where they were given the opportunity to write interactive stories. Older pupils were given a template with a few simple steps to help them in their writing process, in the form of boxes from which the interactive story is built. The development went from having difficulties getting started on their own and writing to using the interactive story to write longer texts with much better content than previously. Several of the pupils also felt that they wanted to try writing different types of texts, and all of a sudden, we had pupils writing poems, short stories, and longer texts.

In the interactive story, it was difficult for the pupils to see the whole, so with the help of cutting the text into a regular writing programme, the pupils became aware of how they developed their abilities in writing texts. And perhaps a combination of pictures and digital tools is the best way. We feel that digital technology contributes to pupils seeing that they are developing and thereby gaining positive experiences, which leads them to dare try new ways of reading, writing, and reporting. Some pupils arrive at our school with low self-esteem and think they cannot develop different skills, like writing texts. If pupils are convinced that their ability is a fixed quality within themselves, the results of schoolwork will be proof of what they can or cannot do (Jonsson, 2024). The assignment gave pupils opportunity to grow and prosper so they could focus on learning writing texts as well as work with their self-efficacy in writing texts.

Interactive quiz

To reduce the stress for our pupils and for them to experience the feeling of success, we started using digital tools in the subject of social studies with older pupils. We wanted to test what the pupils remembered from previous lessons and see what knowledge stuck to use that information in the following lessons.

After a short lecture, pupils had to answer questions in an interactive quiz where different answer options were linked to different questions within the work area. The questions were shown on a large screen in the classroom. We initially read the questions out loud together, but as the pupils felt more confident with the digital tool, they wanted to read by themselves. When they read the question and the different answer options, the pupils had to type in their answers on their mobile devices. We discussed the answers and why the pupils answered the way they did, and in this way, our pupils got to know how others thought. The more we practised, the faster they became with their answers, and we also noticed that pupils began to reflect more on the subject.

When we evaluated the working method together with pupils, they were very satisfied. In addition, the pupils practised more abilities on these occasions, such as reading and understanding what they read, reflecting and thinking critically. The answer options could be a bit tricky, and pupils needed to be alert and think about their answers before answering. Swärd (2024) asks whether pupils are more challenged by not using ready-made material but instead having to create this in collaboration with other pupils. By working together, pupils got a chance to create new knowledge and abilities, which increased their learning as opposed to our giving them a regular test.

Quiz walks with QR codes

Another way to develop our pupils' knowledge and test their knowledge by using digital tools arose when we introduced QR codes into our teaching. At the same time, we were sensitive to the pupils' wishes because they did not want to just to sit down during the lesson – they argued that they would learn more if they didn't sit still all the time in school. Swedish Government Decision (2018) U2018/01430/S says there are studies that show positive connections between physical activity, motor impairment, training, and school performance. This corresponds well with our older pupils' wishes, and we decided to place QR codes at the school, which the pupils in small groups were given the assignment of finding. At the same time, they also had the opportunity to practise looking for information on the internet.

Finding what they were looking for, reading it, and then understanding it was a big step towards independence but also the feeling that knowledge and the ability to learn new things. By finding the QR codes together, pupils had on several occasions also started reasoning, which we could then conclude together in the classroom. Reichenberg (2024) argues that the school has an important task to develop functional literacy so that pupils can develop and become independent in their reading skills.

Virtual reality – VR

When we work with VR in teaching, we use VR glasses, a mobile phone, and a projector connected to a sound system. What is played in the glasses is usually played at the same time on a large screen in the classroom. In this way, we can conduct a dialogue with the pupils to gain a deeper understanding of what they see and experience. During one school year, we worked with the theme "An exciting journey", and some older pupils with severe learning difficulties went by train for a study visit. Before our train trip, we travelled around different countries with the help of digital technology, and through VR technology in the classroom, the pupils got to experience riding the metro. When we then took the train to our study visit, the pupils were able to connect what we had done and experienced with VR technology with their own experiences of the train journey. They reflected, for example, on the fact that it is dark if you go underground with the train because they had seen that in the VR films, and when they rode the metro, the same thing happened. Having experienced and dared to try things via VR before doing it "for real" can calm pupils in a situation, where they would otherwise not have known what will happen. Erstad and Sefton-Green (2012) mention that in order to gain greater understanding of their surroundings, pupils need to be able to move between different places and experience them.

We have visited art museums to see works of art of the great masters which we otherwise would not have had access to. We have also taken walks in several large cities and seen architecture virtually, which gives a completely different experience than looking at pictures in a book. The experience becomes so real that pupils can almost touch and feel the buildings or the paintings hanging in front of them. Imagine not only talking about architecture but also getting to experience it by strolling a street in Rome or walking on the Great Wall of China. Also in this learning process, they get a chance to deepen their understanding of the vocabulary in the subject of art by virtually experiencing the meaning of different words. Wramner and Åkerman (2024) also find it important for pupils to get a concrete meaning of words through study visits so pupils can develop their vocabulary and really understand new words.

Programming

A couple years ago, when we understood that programming was going to be a part of the curriculum, we were a bit confused because none of us knew much about programming. We needed to create a common language and understanding of programming before we started. Based on our experiences, it is important that pupils be allowed to use words in different contexts where they belong in order to gain an increased understanding and be able to use the words in contexts outside school. Swärd (2024) emphasises working with words and their meanings in different ways so pupils can use them in appropriate situations, which in turn also contributes to developing reading comprehension.

By taking part in words and concepts that belong to digital tools, pupils make them natural parts of everyday life. A report from the Swedish parliament (Riksdagen, 2016) describes how digital competence consists of the extent to which one is familiar with digital tools and services and can follow digital development and its impact on one's life. We did find inspiration for our teaching from, among other things, an educational TV programme for beginners in elementary school, where after each programme we could work with similar assignments in the classroom to concretise and create our own experiences. The knowledge was broken down to our pupils' different knowledge levels.

Pupils have worked with words and concepts such as "sequence and bug" by adding patterns and repeating patterns in a sequence. They did this by using, among other things, pipe cleaners, beads, Lego pieces, and pictures. When we laid our sequence, we looked for bugs in the sequences; in this way, the words become natural in the discussions and conversations between us. We also worked to understand that technical objects that are programmed, for example, computers and mobile phones, do not speak our language; they only speak ones and zeros. We made this concrete by turning the lights in the classroom on and off – where zero meant off and one meant on. What does it look like inside the learning board when the pupils write their names? The pupils simply had to test this by writing their names following an ASCII table (the alphabet translated into ones and zeros), and they converted their names into ones and zeroes.

Before we started programming robots or apps, we practised analogue programming by "programming" each other using arrows, which meant that pupils cooperated and communicated with each other by giving each other instructions on how to move around the classroom. At the same time, they practised position words such as straight ahead, straight back, turn right, turn left, etc. If something went wrong in the instruction, a bug appeared – the pupils had to discuss what went wrong and what they should do to make it right. As they worked to develop an understanding of the basics of programming, they also programmed small robots using the same principle as when they programmed themselves. When they mastered this, we went from the concrete to the slightly more abstract by using different programming apps on the learning tablet.

Even more programming

Pupils practise their ability to programme in meaningful situations in combination with knowledge development in various subjects. In these situations, we work with pupils whom we know understand the basics of programming because otherwise it would be difficult to assess if something goes wrong, that is, if it is due to them not having mastered programming or, for example, map skills. Often, pupils are encouraged to work in small groups to be able to discuss together and help each other develop knowledge. We also think, as Persson (2017) writes, that the variations and opportunities it provides make it possible for pupils to take a greater hold on their own learning and can lead to increased commitment and greater motivation among pupils.

Once, our pupils were given the assignment of making a track in transparent plastic that a robot would run on. They pondered and discussed how large the boxes needed to be so that the robot could turn and move only one step in each box, and here the mathematical units of measurement for length came naturally into the teaching. The pupils also had to work with, for example, mental arithmetic in combination with programming. An example of this is when the pupils worked with addition, and they had to calculate, for example, how much two plus two was. They debated the correct answer and collaborated as they then programmed the robot from the starting point to the ending point where the number four was located.

Louvet (2018) believes that the more pupils work with mathematical concepts, the better they can use the concepts to describe what they have done. In the social study subjects, we have worked with the world's continents, and this was perfectly combined with programming. We placed a world map under the track, and the pupils were given the assignment of getting from one continent to another. Other valuable conversations emerged from the discussions where we noticed that pupils reflected on many different things, such as how big our globe is.

Pupils with severe intellectual disabilities wanted to learn English, and one area we chose to work with was colours. We put paper in different colours under the transparent programming mat as well as paper with the names of the colours on it. The students programmed the robot from the red paper to the box where "red" was spelled. Meanwhile, we worked on saying the names of the colours in English so that they learned the pronunciation, and we looked at the spelling combined with seeing the colour. In this assignment, we combined programming with taking advantage of the students' interest in learning English.

In the subject of Swedish, we worked with antonyms that we put under the programming mat, and the pupils programmed the robot from one word to its opposite. Then, we discussed what the words mean in order to gain a deeper knowledge of different words and in what context they can be used. We also wrote sentences using the help of programming a robot, by placing different words that can be combined into sentences under our transparent plastic mat. The pupils had to discuss together which words should be in the sentence and in what order they should be. We then wrote the sentence and programmed the robot so that it moved according to the correct order in the sentence.

When we had worked with programming for a while, we realised that we already used analogue programming in everyday life when we gave instructions and in their schedules. In home and consumer studies, we also work with analogue programming in the form of following recipes. If you don't follow what is written in the recipe, you must look for the "bug" and find out why it didn't turn out as you intended. Pupils have ended up in these situations or that the teacher has been a bit mischievous and deliberately omitted an ingredient, to let pupils figure out where the "bug" is before they start using the recipe. In these situations, pupils get to develop their knowledge, initiative, and creativity.

Summary

Our work with digital tools in Compulsory School for Pupils with Intellectual Disabilities has meant that both the teaching and the pupils learning have developed. The digital tools are used as aids, developing the pupils' literacy in the form of digital storytelling and with the help of interactive stories, and the pupils' knowledge is tested through interactive quizzes and quiz walks with QR codes. Theoretical teaching comes alive with the help of VR technology, and the pupils develop skills and knowledge in programming. But it is important to think about what the purpose of using digital tools is so that they do not just replace pen and paper but rather provide deeper value in teaching.

We strive to have variety in our teaching, and digital tools are part of this. They do not replace other work methods or teaching materials. To be honest, it has not always been easy, and we have had our fair share of problems, but we are getting better as we use them in our teaching because we see the benefits.

References

Andersson, M. (2014). *Berättandets möjligheter – multimodala berättelser och estetiska lärprocesser.* Doktorsavhandling. Luleå tekniska universitet.
Antonovsky, A. (2014). *Natur och Kulturs psykologklassiker – Hälsans mysterium.* Natur och Kultur.
Dweck, C. (2017). *Mindset – du blir vad du tänker.* Natur & Kultur.
Early Learning and Educational Technology Policy Brief. (2016). Retrieved from https://tech.ed.gov/files/2016/10/Early-Learning-Tech-Policy-Brief.pdf
Erstad, O., & Sefton-Green, J. (2012). *Identity, community, and learning lives in the digital age.* Cambridge University Press.
Jonsson, A.-C. (2024). Special educational consequences of implicit notions of ability. In M. Reichenberg, A.-K. Swärd & C. Shipton (Eds.), *Positive special education: Theories, applications and inspiration* (pp. 23–31). Routledge.
Louvet, S. (2018). *Stärk det matematiska självförtroendet: Digitala verktyg i matematikundervisningen.* Gothia Fortbildning.
Ohler, J. B. (2013). *Digital storytelling in the classroom – new media pathways to literacy, learning and creativity.* Corwin Press.
Persson, P. (2017). Tillgänglig utbildning: Är det fel på mig? *Lika värda, 4,* 13.
Reichenberg, M. (2024). Positive special education: Why are teachers' and students' self-efficacy important? Consequences for reading instruction and civic education. In M. Reichenberg, A.-K. Swärd & C. Shipton (Eds.), *Positive special education: Theories, applications and inspiration* (pp. 7–22). Routledge.
Riksdagen. (2016). *Digitaliseringen i skolan – dess påverkan på kvalitet, likvärdighet och resultat i utbildningen* (2015/2016: RFR18). Retrieved from https://data.riksdagen.se/fil/24B42258-6038-470F-80C6-F5CE149F401B
Shipton, C. (2024). Inclusive literacy: Film, visuals, and creative writing – The facts in the case of Mister Hollow. In M. Reichenberg, A.-K. Swärd & C. Shipton (Eds.), *Positive special education: Theories, applications and inspiration* (pp. 77–87). Routledge.
Swärd, A.-K. (2024). Positive special education: Challenge students to read and write in a creative way without fixed material. In M. Reichenberg, A.-K. Swärd & C. Shipton (Eds.), *Positive special education: Theories, applications and inspiration* (pp. 95–103). Routledge.
Swedish Government Decision. (2018). U2018/01430/S. *Uppdrag om mer rörelse i skolan.* Retrieved from https://www.regeringen.se/regeringsuppdrag/2018/04/uppdrag-om-mer-rorelse-i-skolan
Wood, D., Bruner, J., & Ross, G. (1976). The role of tutoring in problem solving. *Journal of Child Psychology and Psychiatry, 17,* 89–100.
Wramner, L., & Åkerman, A.-K. (2024). The Witting method – Safe, creative, and without textbook. In M. Reichenberg, A.-K. Swärd & C. Shipton (Eds.), *Positive special education: Theories, applications and inspiration* (pp. 131–141). Routledge.

7 Teaching expressive communication to pupils with SEND

Georgiana Woodcock

In this chapter, I will explore adaptive teaching and consider an optimistic approach to inclusion by thinking about how to effectively meet the needs of all pupils in one lesson. The chapter is based on work at Archdale School, which is a school for children aged 3 to 11 with special educational needs and is located in Sheffield, England. The lesson described in this chapter was taught to pupils, with both moderate and severe learning difficulties, in a mixed Key Stage 1 and Key Stage 2 class with the pupils aged 6 to 11. The pupils in the class have a range of special needs such as autism, communication difficulties, Down syndrome, cerebral palsy, and complex medical needs. The pupils are from a range of backgrounds, and one child has English as an additional language.

Archdale School has three curriculum pathways, which include the Early Years Foundation Stage, Informal Curriculum, and Semi-Formal Curriculum. Initially, the pathways were based upon the Equals Curriculum (Equals, 2022) but have been adapted to meet the needs of the schools learning community. All of the pupils discussed in this chapter is working on a Semi-Formal Curriculum, but there is a continuum from the earliest stages of the pathway up to those who are working towards a more Formal Curriculum. At Archdale School, the curriculum enables teachers to plan and deliver personalised teaching and learning experiences to meet pupils' individual learning needs. When planning teaching and learning experiences, teachers see each pupil as an individual and focus on what they can currently do and have already achieved. Teachers will then build on pupils' prior learning through effective learning sequences to ensure pupils experience success and have repeated opportunities to achieve the knowledge or skill being taught.

One of the complexities of teaching children with special educational needs and disabilities in both specialist and mainstream education settings is that learning needs of the pupils can vary so significantly. I will look at a communication lesson in depth, which focuses on the teaching of expressive communication. The National Literacy Trust (2004, p.19) state, "Expressive language is defined as speaking and any communication production that is both verbal or through gestures". It is important to develop expressive communication skills because literacy, communication, and language underpin all aspects of

DOI: 10.4324/9781003509141-7

the curriculum and enable individuals to connect and communicate with others. Expressive communication looks different for each pupil in the classroom. For example, one pupil might be learning to act intentionally to gain attention by guiding an adult to something they want whilst another pupil is learning to sequence words to form written sentences. It is our aim as teachers to find ways for pupils to feel included in a lesson regardless of what they are working on and to have access to resources.

Adaptive teaching

In England and Wales, the Teachers' Standards (Department for Education, 2011) set out eight standards, which teachers must uphold in their teaching practice, alongside professional and personal conduct. Teacher standard 5 (TS5) is "Adapts teaching to respond to the strengths and needs of all pupils", which incorporates how to adapt teaching appropriately and having a clear understanding of the needs of all pupils including those with SEND. Alternatively, The Department for Education (2019) set out the Early Career Framework, which is a document which considers the support teachers should receive in the early stages of their career. It considers adaptive teaching as part of the framework. Eaton writes in a blog for the Education Endowment Foundation (2022) that adaptive teaching is about being responsive and adjusting teaching to match our pupil's needs. In the following lesson, I used adaptive teaching by adapting the task given to pupils, adjusting the level of adult support provided and incorporating ICT. Alternatively, the teaching strategies used to deliver the main part of the lesson were in response to my knowledge of what would engage the pupils in their learning. When working with pupils with SEND, it is important to have an optimistic approach to inclusion and be able to use adaptive teaching whilst maintaining high expectations of all pupils. It is paramount to have a thorough knowledge of the pupils and understanding how teaching can be adapted to ensure every pupil can succeed in the lesson, which is linked to positive special education. Seligman et al., (2009) talk about education for both traditional skills and for happiness. Literacy, language, and communication underpin all aspects of the curriculum and life and enable pupils to connect and communicate with others.

The lesson

The lesson was taught to ten pupils, and lessons would typically last 45 minutes. Lessons include a combination of whole-class activities, small group activities, and some individual tasks. For the starter activity, the whole-class participated in a sensory story which linked to our termly topic "All About Me and My Community". I had written a non-fiction story called "People Who Help", which required the pupils to listen to a description and look at pictures and sensory props related to different jobs in the community and guess who they thought the person might be. For example, there were descriptions,

Learning objectives	Activities
Group 1: To use talk to organise, sequence, and clarify thinking before writing a sentence to describe a picture.	Write a sentence to describe a picture linked to the topic "People who help us".
Group 2: To begin to form letter type shapes to write words to describe pictures.	Write words and practise letter formation to describe pictures linked to the topic "People who help us".
Group 3: To begin to form letter-type shapes to write initial sounds to describe pictures.	Identify initial sound for the picture and trace or copy letter to practise letter formation.
Group 4: To type initial sound letters to describe pictures.	Identify initial sound for the picture, locate letter on the keyboard, and type it.
Group 5: To respond in ways which could be interpreted as a deliberate request for more and to share attention briefly.	Attention autism bucket activity.

props, and pictures related to police officers, teachers, firefighters, dentists, and doctors. In this lesson, the sensory story provided a context and purpose for the pupils writing as the writing task was linked to one of the jobs they had explored in the story. Sensory stories are a positive way to immerse pupils into a topic and can provide a group learning experience. Within one sensory story, objectives can be adapted to meet the learning needs of a wide range of pupils. For some pupils it provides an opportunity to respond to and explore different sensory props. For other pupils, they might develop key vocabulary linked to the topic or develop their understanding and comprehension by answering questions about what they have heard.

For the main part of the lesson, pupils were split into small groups or worked individually with an adult to complete an expressive communication activity. A possible way of describing a successful lesson in positive special education is one which incorporates adaptive teaching, has an optimistic approach, high expectations, and ensures learning is personalised to meet pupils' individual learning needs. I group pupils depending on the outcome I want them to achieve in the lesson and ensure an adult is available to work with each group to guide and model learning.

- Group 1 consisted of two pupils who are working towards a formal curriculum. They were given a picture of a vet scenario and asked to verbally dictate a sentence before writing it. The pupils discussed with an adult what they could see in the picture and how they could translate that into a coherent sentence (Figure 7.1 and Figure 7.2).
- Group 2 and 3 consisted of five pupils who are focusing on letter formation (Figure 7.3 and Figure 7.4).

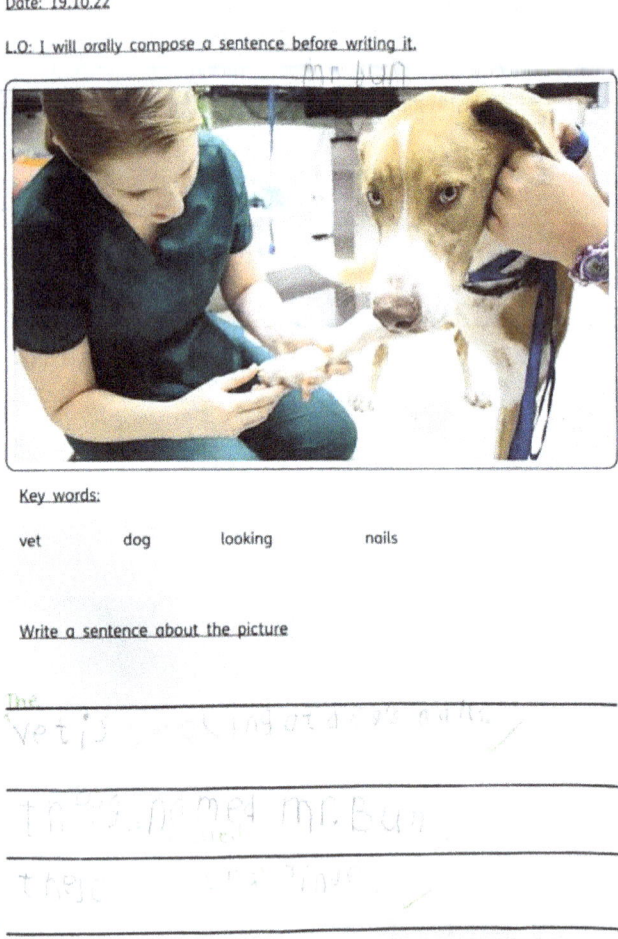

Figure 7.1 Using keywords to compose a sentence

The pupil in Figure 7.1 was given keywords to support her initial sentence. Providing keywords supported the pupil to construct an initial sentence about the picture. She wrote "Vet is looking at dog's nails". She was then challenged to write two more sentences about the picture. She wrote, "The dog named Mr Bun" and "The dog's colour ginger".

Teaching expressive communication to pupils with SEND 67

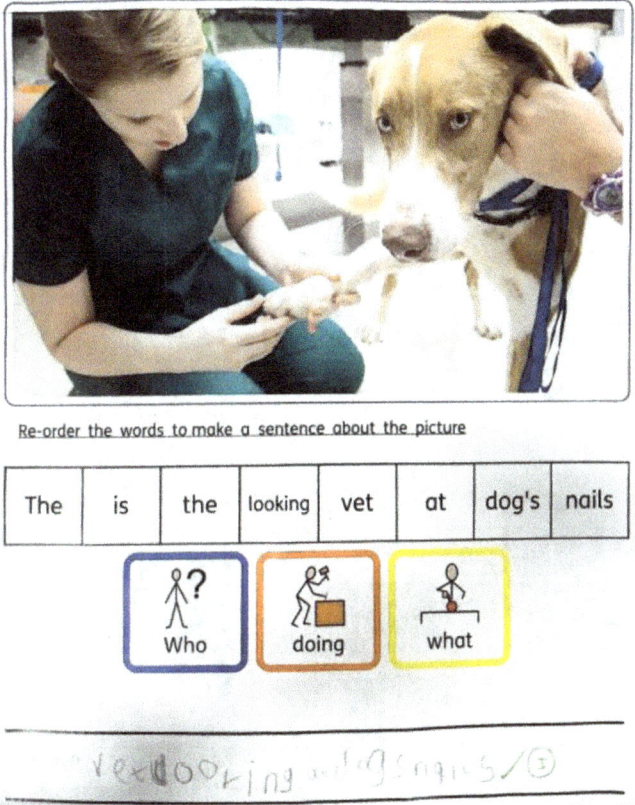

Figure 7.2 Placing the words in the correct order

Source: © Widgit Software Ltd 2002–2024. www.widgit.com.

The pupil in Figure 7.2 was given a sentence which needed unscrambling and a sentence maker visual prompt. Sentence makers or colourful semantics support pupils understanding of sentence structure. The pupil used the sentence maker to construct the sentence "The vet looking at dogs nails". The pupil was then prompted to use all of the given words and wrote the sentence, "The vet is looking at the dogs nails".

Figure 7.3 Writing the correct words to match the photographs

Source: © Widgit Software Ltd 2002–2024. www.widgit.com.

Figure 7.3 shows the work of a pupil who can form recognisable letters and is beginning to copy words. He used the keywords at the top of the sheet to support his spelling when writing the captions for the pictures.

Teaching expressive communication to pupils with SEND 69

Figure 7.4 Forming letters

Source: © Widgit Software Ltd 2002–2024. www.widgit.com.

Figure 7.4 shows the work of a pupil who is developing her letter formation skills. She looked at the picture and identified what it was. She then traced over the initial letter and then attempted to copy it independently.

Figure 7.5 Locating the letters on the keyboard and typing

Source: © Widgit Software Ltd 2002–2024. www.widgit.com.

Figure 7.5 shows the same task, but it has been differentiated to incorporate technology to ensure it is accessible for the pupil. The pupil is learning to locate letters on a keyboard to be able to independently write the initial letters. The pupil worked 1:1 with an adult to look at the picture, identify what was happening in them, and then attempt to find the initial letter with increasing independence.

Teaching expressive communication to pupils with SEND 71

Figure 7.6 Exciting toys

Figure 7.6 shows the three exciting toys from the bucket which were explored as part of stage 1 during Attention Autism. One of the toys used was a spinning top, and one of the pupils leaned forward in his chair to get a closer look.

- Group 4 was made up of one pupil who is developing his use of ICT to support his independent writing skills (Figure 7.5).
- Group 5 consisted of two pupils who were developing their shared attention skills and communicating a deliberate request for more of something through an Attention Autism session. Attention Autism is an approach founded by Gina Davies (see Davies, 2013–2024) and consists of four stages: stage 1: focus; stage 2: sustain; stage 3: shift; and stage 4: 1,2,3 and transitions. The two pupils in this group participated in stage 1 and stage 2. Stage 1 required the pupils to focus on three exciting toys from the bucket. During stage 2, the adult used a sponge and red, yellow, green, and blue paint to create a rainbow. The pupils focused their attention on the activity and sustained it for the duration (Figure 7.6).

For the plenary, most of the pupils were encouraged to complete an independent activity which was linked to the main part of the lesson. For pupils who an independent activity was not appropriate for, they had some time to support and manage their emotional regulation by accessing an activity of their choice. Most of the pupils had a choice to either trace the alphabet or to write it independently, depending on how confident they felt. This enabled pupils to practise the skills they had learned in the session and gave them autonomy over the task they chose to do. It also supported their independence skills as they needed to collect their own activities and the resources needed to complete it.

Comments

Overall, the lesson was a success because positive special education was used, the adults had high expectations of their pupils, all the pupils engaged in their specific learning activities and worked towards their intended objectives of developing their expressive communication skills. The lesson was also effective because the learning objectives and planned activities were carefully planned to meet the pupil's individual needs, but it also provided a challenge. By pitching the lesson carefully and finding a balance between challenging and achievable, pupils were able to practise their writing skills in a familiar context and develop their mindset around their writing ability by accomplishing the task.

References

Davies, G. (2013–2024). *Gina Davies Autism Centre*. Retrieved from https://www.ginadavies.co.uk

Department for Education. (2011). *Teachers' standards*. Retrieved January 31, 2023, from https://assets.publishing.service.gov.uk/government/uploads/system/uploads/attachment_data/file/665522/Teachers_standard_information.pdf

Department for Education. (2019). *Early career framework*. Retrieved January 31, 2023, from https://assets.publishing.service.gov.uk/government/uploads/system/uploads/attachment_data/file/978358/Early-Career_Framework_April_2021.pdf

Education Endowment Foundation. (2022). *Guest blog: Jon Eaton, Director of Kingsbridge Research School and Research Lead at Kingsbridge Community College, reflects on what adaptive teaching has meant for their trust, education southwest.* Retrieved January 31, 2023, from https://educationendowmentfoundation.org.uk/news/moving-from-differentiation-to-adaptive-teaching

Equals. (2022). *Semi-formal Curriculum SLD/MLD.* Retrieved January 31, 2023, from https://equals.co.uk/equals-semi-formal-curriculum-sld-curriculum/

National Literacy Trust. (2004). *Television and language development in the early years: A review of the literature.* Retrieved April 4, 2023, from https://cdn.literacytrust.org.uk/media/documents/2004_04_01_free_research_-_television_and_early_language_development_review_DXQ8Gw1.pdf

Seligman, M. E. P., Ernst, R. M., Gillham, J., Reivich, K., & Linkins, M. (2009). Positive education: Positive psychology and classroom interventions. *Oxford Review of Education, 35,* 293–311.

8 Teaching functional literacy to pupils with SEN

Matt Maguire

Functional applications of literacy in the community

Pupils with special educational needs, whatever their need, have a right to experience and access the world around them. This includes not just their home environment but also the local community. This though is an environment in which we are surrounded by words, symbols, and other visual stimuli which require an element of literacy to understand.

Whether it is in knowing which shop to buy bread versus a lightbulb, knowing which bus or train to take to get home or working out how to go about sending a letter, literacy is required for all. That is even before we look at the huge amount of speaking and listening skills required to effectively make almost any transaction in the community.

In order to be able to access their communities, all pupils with SEN will benefit from tools to solve these problems, and that is why functional literacy is vital to effective and safe community access.

Class context

The group of pupils for the activities detailed next is a mixed ability Post 16 group, comprising pupils aged between 16–18 and with a range of educational needs, from MLD to SLD, including a number on the autistic spectrum. In terms of their previous understanding of literacy, some pupils are able to read, write, and communicate effectively, while others cannot read or write and have limited verbal communication. All however have a right to access their community.

The community in this context being London, specifically the London Borough of Camden. A key aspect of life in London is being able to get around safely, without using cars or taxis. Of the class of 13 pupils, 6 are currently independent travellers, so they travel to and from school each morning on their own, without being given lifts by parents or by local authority transport.

Becoming an independent traveller is a great source of pride for pupils at Swiss Cottage as it has a huge effect on pupils' confidence, autonomy, and morale. It often has even more of an effect on the parents however as they begin to see that their son or daughter has the potential to live safely and more independently than they had previously envisaged.

DOI: 10.4324/9781003509141-8

Travel Training therefore is a key part of the Post 16 curriculum at Swiss Cottage School and was the focus of this lesson. Specifically on planning and finding routes to new locations.

Route planning and finding in zone 1

Day and time

Tuesday Morning 9:45 a.m.–12:00 p.m.

Learning intentions

- I will use Google Maps to plan a route to a new place (MLD learners).
- I will match up tube lines to their colours (SLD learners).
- I will use a route plan to safely find my way to a new place (MLD learners).
- I will use visual cues, symbols, and colour codes to safely find my way to a new place (SLD learners).

Lesson plan

This lesson is divided into two distinct halves. Firstly a classroom session of 45 minutes for route planning. This is followed by 90 minutes of community learning for pupils to work together to find the route they have planned.

For the first session, the group is divided roughly into two, between those who are more ICT literate, able to use Google Maps effectively, and those who cannot. The aim is to make every activity meaningful and realistic. Some learners are not at the point where they are able to effectively use a computer without 1:1 support, so there is little point in having a TA plan the route for them. More meaningful is to find a mechanism through which those pupils can independently engage with the concept of route planning – this is done through learning the colour codes of the tube lines.

Planning activity for ICT literate pupils

The previous worksheet gives a clear structure for more able pupils. Requiring them to read and also use their ICT skills to solve the problem presented to them, of how to find a route using public transport in London.

Skills utilised in this activity are as follows: reading, in order to follow the instructions correctly; writing, to accurately copy down the correct route in a manner which is accessible; ICT skills, to correctly use the technology of Google Maps to find the route.

More independent pupils follow these instructions independently and the teacher checks on these pupils throughout the lesson to check on their learning. Any less able pupils may be supported by a teaching assistant working 1:1 or with a pair of pupils at the same computer.

Journey Planning and Route Finding

What is this ship called?

    Mayflower   Titanic   Cutty Sark   QE2

Where is it in London?

    Camden   Greenwich   Islington   Brixton

Try finding the location by searching in google.

What is the postcode?   _____

Figure 8.1 Find the name on this ship

Teaching functional literacy to pupils with SEN 77

Planning your route Back to School

- We will be travelling there by River Boat but need to plan the journey back to school after we leave.

- Click on the Maps tab in your google window

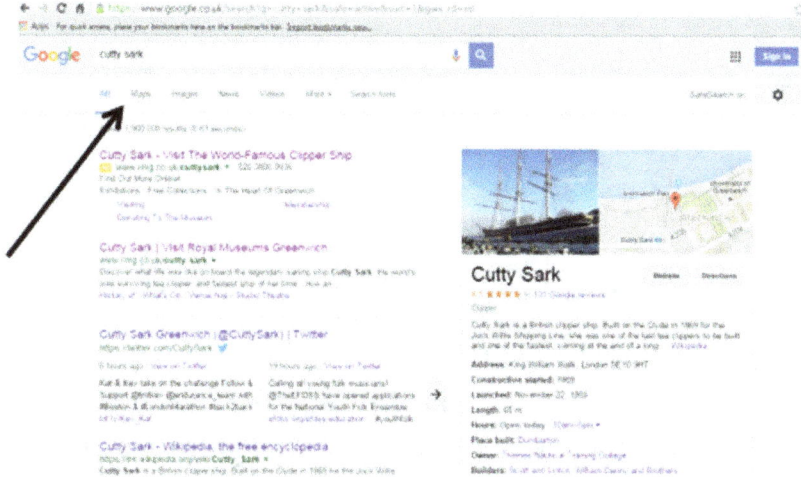

- Now click on Directions

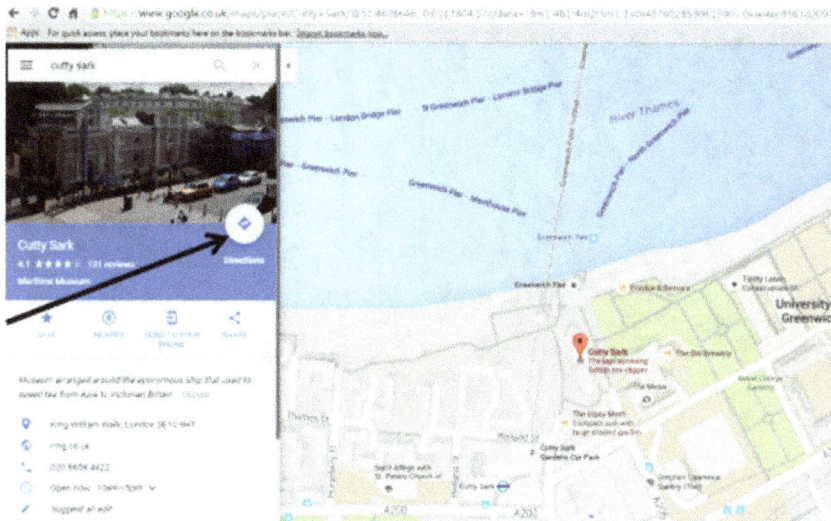

Figure 8.2 Planning your route back to school
Source: Google Maps.

78 *Positive Special Education*

- Type "Swiss Cottage" as your starting point and click on the little picture of a train

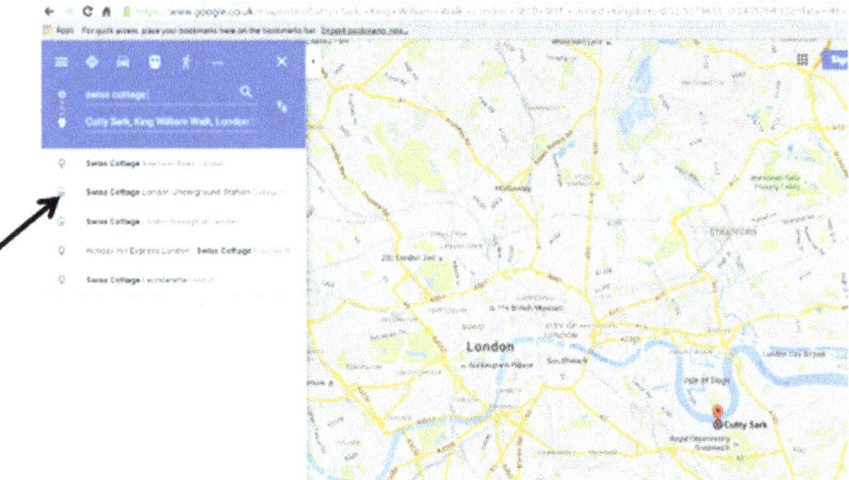

- This now shows you a driving route. You need to tell it to find you a public transport route. Click on the little train symbol.

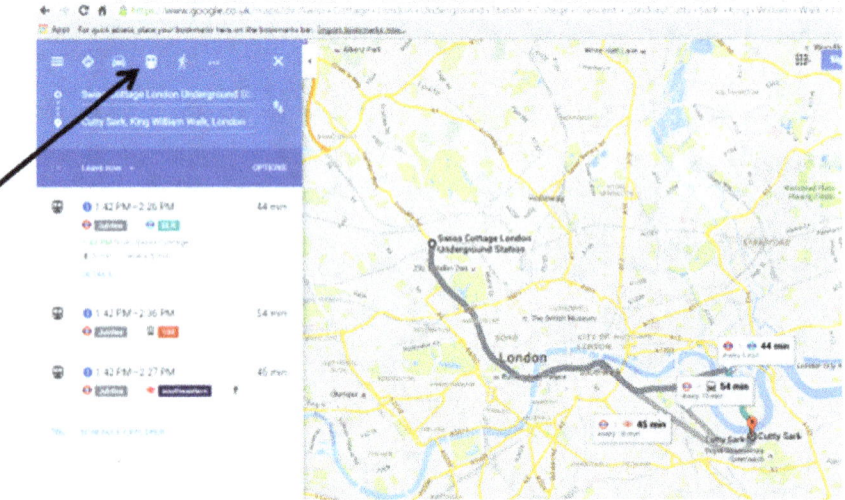

Figure 8.3 Find a public transport route
Source: Google Maps.

Teaching functional literacy to pupils with SEN 79

- The route showing is the wrong direction. Click the little arrows to switch direction.

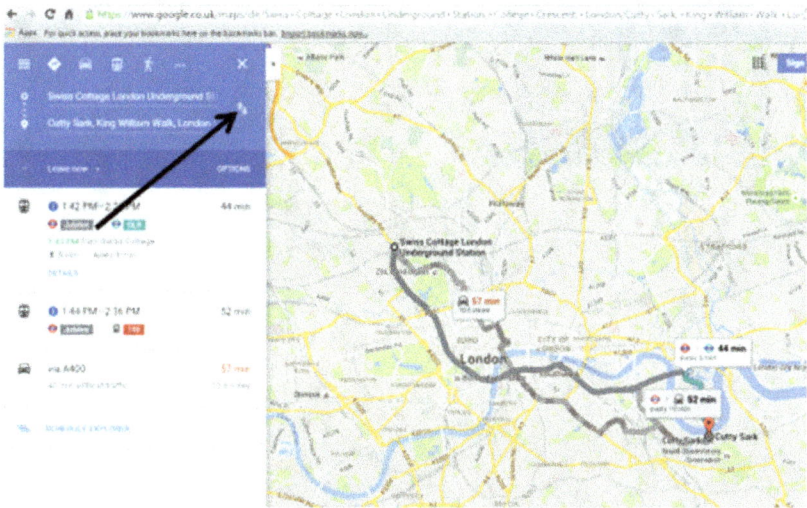

- You need change the day and time. Click where it says "Leave now" and change to "Depart at"

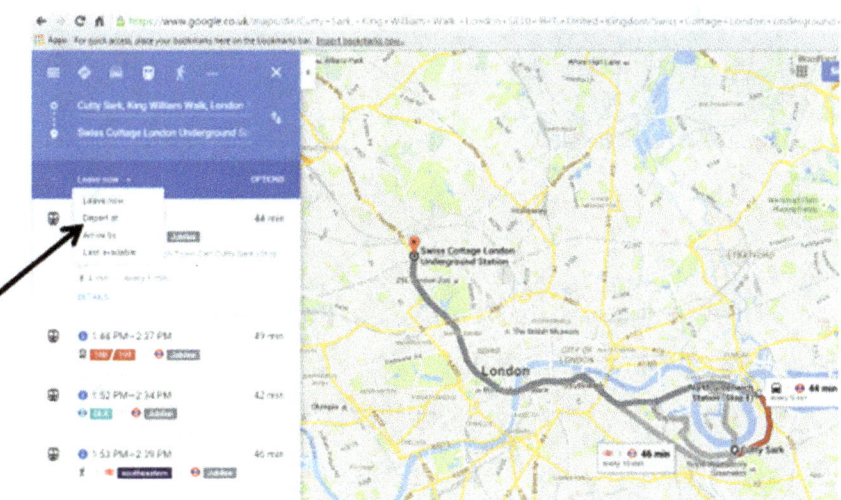

Figure 8.4 Change day and time or direction
Source: Google Maps.

80 *Positive Special Education*

- Change the time to 2:00PM on Wed, Mar 9

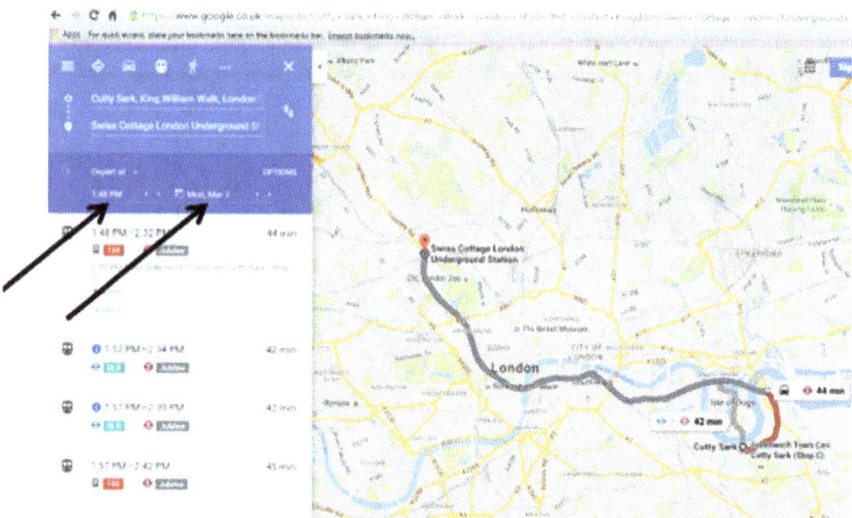

- This now shows your journey options. Click on one for more details

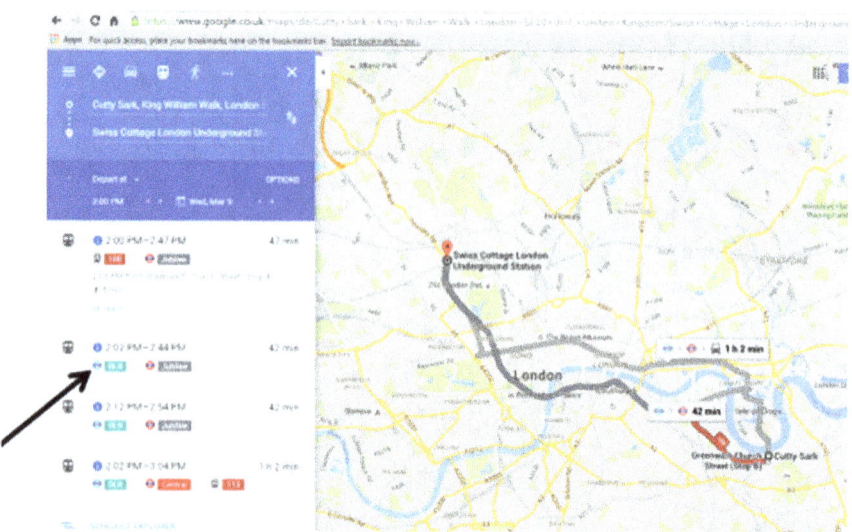

- Copy down the details of your chosen route below over the page.

Figure 8.5 Change time
Source: Google Maps.

The aim of the activity is for each pupil to have accurately written down the optimum route for the journey within 30 minutes of the lesson starting. This group of learners will then sit together to share their routes, developing speaking and listening skills, before negotiating as a group which route they would follow to reach their destination. This group would then depart with a teaching assistant to follow their agreed route.

Planning activity for SLD pupils

Figure 8.6 Colours of the tube lines in the London Underground

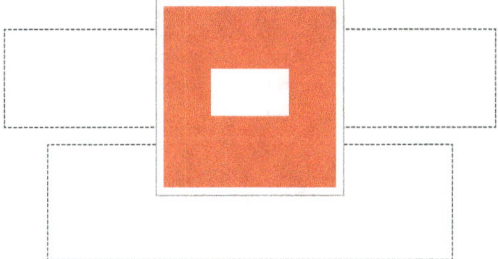

Figure 8.7 An example of a tube line in the London Underground

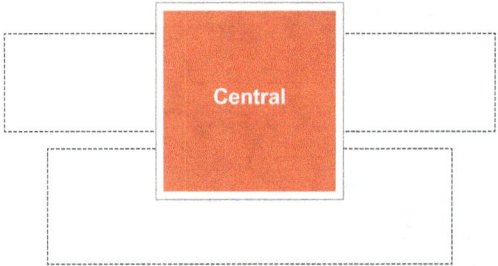

Figure 8.8 Central tube line

82 *Positive Special Education*

For SLD learners the focus is on them learning the colours for each tube line as they are all clearly labelled and colour coded, allowing pupils who cannot read to still recognise which line is which and find their way around the network.

The activity begins with each colour being shown and then revealing which line that colour represents as seen previously. This is repeated, and no hands questioning is used to reinforce the learning.

After all the lines have been repeated, the final slide is a drag and drop activity with pupils taking turns to drag the correct name of each line to its representative colour.

Pupils then complete a worksheet, supported by a teaching assistant if necessary, to demonstrate their understanding of the colours for each tube line.

In order to plan their route, pupils use a large print tube map, which is on a wall in the classroom, to follow the tube lines from their origin to their destination and copy down the colours of the lines they will take to get there.

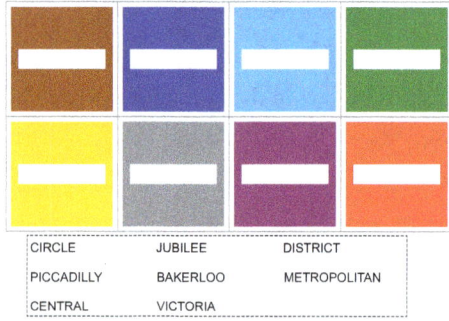

Figure 8.9 Match the name of each underground line to the correct colour

Figure 8.10 Write the name of each underground line next to the corresponding colour

Practical activity for all pupils

The second part of this lesson is the practical element, with pupils following their agreed route to find their destination. With a group of six students, they will be accompanied by two teaching assistants, but their role is very much hands off. Students are encouraged to communicate with each other and problem solve their way through the transport network, following their agreed route, which will be printed off and taken with them.

The role of the teaching assistants is to follow the group from a distance of approximately 10–20 metres, not interfering with the pupils even if they make a mistake and take a wrong direction. The teaching assistant may suggest problem-solving strategies such as asking for help, or checking their route plan again, but specific direction how to correct the error is not given.

The other role of the teaching assistant is to ensure all pupils in the group are included in the route finding, by targeting questions to quieter members of the group at key points in the journey, such as checking their understanding of the different tube lines, as practised in the classroom part of the lesson.

During this community-based practical, pupils will need to demonstrate a range of literacy skills such as reading their route plan, train and station signage, and speaking and listening skills when problem solving with each other or asking members of the public or transport staff for help.

Once the group has reached their destination, the teaching assistants will ask targeted questions to the group about the route they had taken and the decisions made along the way, with the aim to formatively assess each pupil's understanding and progress. If needed, the teaching assistants may state that different pupils need to take the lead on the return journey to school, ensuring that the bulk of the route finding work is not done by one or two individuals in the group.

If the group gets a long way off course and is not going to successfully make it back to school in time, the teaching assistants can abort the journey and return with the group back to school for a review of what went wrong, with this same journey then attempted again the following week.

Summary of learning

In conclusion, the primary objective of this lesson is to develop pupils' confidence and independence in the community, specifically when travelling around London's complex and busy transport network. It recognises though that this is fundamentally dependent on elements of functional literacy. As such, the lesson incorporates reading, writing, speaking, and listening and the use of ICT within its activities.

The community-based practical session then provides an ideal assessment opportunity to see how much real learning has been attained by the pupils. The role of the teaching assistants in this regard is crucial to ensure that the activity is genuinely being led by pupils and that all pupils have opportunities to demonstrate their understanding.

The aim is for all students who are part of this lesson to become more independent, one day becoming independent travellers if they are not already, who are confident to go out into their communities, accessing the world around them, regardless of the barriers which they face.

9 Inclusive literacy

Film, visuals, and creative writing –
The Facts in the Case of Mister Hollow

Catherine Shipton

Figure 9.1 A Character from *The Facts in the Case of Mister Hollow*
Source: © Permission from Someone at the Door Productions.

In this chapter I will demonstrate how to use film as a tool to support the development of speaking and listening, and reading and writing skills. I highlight this within the context of a lesson involving a group of teenagers with moderate learning difficulties. I will demonstrate how to include all of the class using film, targeting a range of aspects of literacy development from early emergent writing and reading to the use of more complex language and extended writing. I will show how the same piece of visual literacy can be used to target different areas of literacy development within the same classroom and effectively include a range of learning needs.

Film evokes visualisation and captures interest. We hold different opinions about the same piece of film. Film can engage pupils and inspire their imagination, creativity, and thinking around the characters, the plot, and the meanings of the films watched. The open-ended nature of film allows pupils to tackle writing differently, in ways that are individual to them: risks can be taken, and the content can be more pupil-specific since our responses are different. There is no wrong

DOI: 10.4324/9781003509141-9

or right in our responses to film, and it is this open-endedness that is desirable: pupils are not scared of making a mistake or getting the wrong answer. Once we have captured the imagination of the pupil and engaged them, we can focus on specific literacy skills and genuinely personalise and adapt the learning.

I will use the example of *The Facts in the Case of Mister Hollow*, a short award-winning film directed by **Gudiño and Marcone** and released in July 2008. The film has minimal words, other than in the introductory sequences. Eerie music is played, and thought-provoking images based around a changing black-and-white photograph are shown. The camera captures these as it zooms in and out, focusing on different aspects of the scene or the people there. What has happened in the film is unclear, and the viewer is left with a sense of uncertainty, suspense, and wonder: the pupils can communicate this in a number of ways, which we can explore further by setting out ideas in the means of a lesson plan.

The described lesson has been used with teenagers from 12 to 16 years old, all of whom had been identified as having a learning difficulty. This can vary, but typically they would be described as having moderate learning difficulties. The pupils at the time all attended a day special school and had an Educational Health Care Plan for their learning difficulties. Many of them had specific difficulties with literacy and were at the early stages of reading and writing. Some used repetitive and familiar phrases mostly, while others engaged in complex conversations. Some of the young people came from homes where English was an additional language. All pupils experienced some anxiety at times about their learning and required support to boost their confidence, while many also required support to focus their attention for prolonged periods of time. What has been remarkable in using film is the way that pupils have engaged with the film and thrown away inhibitions. The visual nature and the intriguing content makes this a film that has the potential to reach pupils with more complex needs, as well as can be used with an even wider variety of pupils than shown here.

Overview of the lesson content and structure

A typical lesson would last one hour. In the initial session, approach the lesson with an approximate structure as set out in Figure 9.2:

---

i. Watch the short film (6 minutes)
ii. Invite responses and questions (2-3 minutes gathering initial reactions)
iii. Discuss as a class the content of the film using Who? What? Why? Where? How? Questions. The complexity of questions can vary (5 minutes) moving from closed to open-ended questions (see Figure 1b)
iv. Watch the film for a second time, pausing to pose questions and gather observations (10 minutes), gaining more detail and gathering more information and evidence about what has happened
v. Complete a written activity (30 – 35 minutes)

Figure 9.2 Lesson structure

The entire sequence of activities in the lesson structure could be completed in one sitting depending on the pupils in the class. On each viewing of this particular film more detail is gathered, and further viewings of the same film provoke further analyses and learning opportunities to delve deeper, to pose questions and establish opinions, sustain participation, and develop the complexity of learning. Alternatively, the theme of the film could be the catalyst for a series of extended sessions, each with a different focus, for example, see Figure 9.4 for further ideas for activities. I will highlight here how this film could be used to sequence and retell the events depicted in the film and show how different learning areas can be addressed simultaneously, how visual literacy can be used to promote inclusive teaching and promote positive special education.

Capture the interest of the class: begin by playing the film and allow the pupils to watch and observe and be captivated by what is happening. Allow the pupils time to reflect on what they have viewed before collecting their thoughts and their questions and gather their responses. The content is relevant, provocative, and accessible to a teenager. It has an element of mystery which is appealing. Because there are no right and wrong answers and it is unclear what has happened in the film, the students are enthused to offer suggestions and develop their speaking and listening skills without fear of giving an incorrect answer. Teenagers who are otherwise conscious of their literacy ability are inspired (see also Ann-Katrin Sward's chapter). They can speak freely and try and figure out the sequence of events and the motives.

Questions, questioning, and attention to detail

After watching the film for the first time, the pupils want to ask questions. The teacher poses questions that are directed at different pupils in the class, reflecting different abilities, always allowing time for responses and not interjecting with definitive replies. The teacher must allow a sense that every answer is relevant since the film is full of uncertainties and the pupils are interpreting the same piece of film in different ways. The pupils need to own their discussions, and the teacher must skilfully pause as well as question further. Questions that you could ask are set out in Figure 9.3 and are a fantastic way of assessing immediately how the pupils have perceived what they have viewed and how they have decoded some of the images. This decoding of the images is in itself a valuable learning experience.

The amount of discussion that you allow will depend on the class, and the teacher can decide how to structure this part of the session. In my classes I let the pupils lead the discussion. The teacher might encourage whole class responses, or paired or group conversations. The objective of questioning is to allow for assessment for learning opportunities and to encourage links to be made, both in the film and in pupils' thinking. Speaking and listening skills can be developed as the class develop reasoning skills as well as naming and using vocabulary to label what they have seen, or the emotions that might have been evoked in response to the film, or as interpreted by the characters in the images. Pupils gain a confidence in speaking as they develop a sense of capability and self-efficacy (see Monica Reichenberg's chapter).

88 *Positive Special Education*

	Increasing complexity of questioning →	
Questions with forced	Closed questions	Open questions
Is the scene set at night or day? Is the scene in a churchyard or a supermarket?	Who is in the photograph? What is the woman holding? What is the woman wearing?	What has happened? Who do you think the characters are? Why is there a body in the car? Who do you think the car belongs to? How do you know that it is night? How is the woman feeling?

Figure 9.3 Questions

After watching the film, posing initial questions, and gauging the reactions of the class, play the film again. This time around, pause the film and draw attention to detail. Ask questions to encourage the class to consider closer observation and to encourage them to think beyond what they can see, making inferences and establishing links. Pause the film and draw attention to key evidence such as the tattoos on the men's wrists or the ring on the finger of the hand in the car. Don't tell the class what they are looking at, but ask them to tell you what they can see. Create an interest and excitement: What can you see? What has changed? Do you think the woman is excited, or is she scared? Why, etc. Using film allows for changing perceptions. It draws the viewer in and enables a decoding of visual images in a way that is appropriate to the learner.

The shared exploration of film allows for different perspectives to be addressed and for the development of evidence-based arguments potentially. The pupils are able in this particular example to give a voice to the silent moving images that are so powerful on the screen, give power to their own ideas, and give power to their own voice.

Lesson activities and links to learning intentions

I will outline a typical example of the variety of activities that were completed in my lesson and which addressed a variety and range of learning needs. Figure 9.4 shows the activities covered in one lesson using the same film and, with the overriding aim of retelling what has been viewed, developing word,

Learning Intentions	Activity	Area addressed
a) To develop understanding and use of questions	Encourage the pupils to formulate questions about the film content using question words. Pose a variety of questions about the content of the film for the pupils to answer (encouraging them to use direct one-word answers to full and complex sentences) Pupils should capture the questions and write down the questions that have been generated or record them. Pupils should answer the questions that have been generated orally and / or in writing.	Sentence level Speaking and listening
b) To read (and write) key words	Use frames from the film to support pupils to write key words that have been seen in the picture, e.g. man, baby, or to match key words or key symbols to pictures from the film	Word level
c) To structure a sentence To describe what they have seen	Get pupils to read a simple sentence and match it to an associated photograph. Ask pupils to read a selection of words and put them together to create a sentence related to the film. Use sentence makers to help pupils to build and create sentences. Ask pupils to write a simple sentence to go with a picture from the film	Word level Sentence level
d) To sequence events	Use a set of photographs and stills and ask pupils to sequence them in the order that they appeared in the film. Sequence a set of pictures from the film	Text level
e) To retell a sequence of events	Ask pupils to sequence a set of pictures from the film. Use the pictures to help retell each part of the film's story using sentences. Have a word bank available to support pupils where necessary.	Text level
f) To use paragraphs and complex sentences To make inferences	Use the photographs from the film and ask pupils to retell their own version of events to create a short story or narrative. Encourage pupils to use increasingly detailed and complex sentences and paragraphs. Have pupils use a dictionary or spellcheck to check spellings and encourage them to use a thesaurus to include interesting words.	Word level Sentence level Text level

Figure 9.4 Learning intentions and activities for lesson

sentence, and text level reading and writing skills. The main activity was to take a set of frames which told the story of aspects of the film, to support the pupils in retelling the film.

Specific activities

Figures 9.1, 9.5 and 9.10 are stills from the film. A set of anything between 4 and 16 stills could be used, depending on the complexity and detail you want the young people to include, for retelling the film. The examples demonstrate the different levels of literacy that can be addressed using the same, engaging content. Figure 9.5 is the first of a series of stills which the class went on to use to retell but illustrates how young people who are not yet able to read are included in the lesson too. The pictures could be used individually also, to evoke language from the pupils to describe what is happening.

Pupil 1 matches the symbols to the images in the film stills. They are very interested in the content, and so this encourages their participation with the task, which is working on reading skills at a very early level without compromising the subject content of the film:

Pupil 1 is developing an understanding that text carries meaning and is developing symbol recognition. This pupil required support to focus their attention.

Pupil 2 writes the words *man, woman, car, baby* underneath (see Figure 9.6). Pupil 2 is working on picking out the key information from the picture. They can name key people and items and are beginning to sound out phonetically to write common words. The work is kept focused and linked to the pictures to support concentration and self-confidence.

Figure 9.5 A scene from *The Facts in the Case of Mister Hollow* to visualise the film
Source: © Permission from Someone at the Door Productions.

Figure 9.6 Four keywords and symbols
Source: © Widgit Software Ltd 2002–2024. www.widgit.com.

Inclusive literacy 91

Pupil 3 reads through a symbolised sentence then matches the words, developing their reading of keywords. They can then have a go at copywriting the words and developing pencil control. Again, the pupil is able to develop early literacy skills while still using subject matter and resources that are appealing to the teenager.

Pupil 4: This pupil uses approaches based on sentence makers to support them to structure and order keywords through colour coding:

Pupil 5 dictates a sentence, *There was a woman holding a baby*, which is scribed for the pupil and which they then overwrite and read back. They could also type this sentence.

Pupil 6 reads through the following cut up words: *man The had hat. a* and puts them back together to make a sentence: The man had a hat.

The pupil is interested in the picture and is talking about it. They can identify a few keywords in text and are now beginning to develop more structural sequencing of a sentence. Over time this builds up with complexity of structure and of words.

Pupil 7 writes a sentence themselves that they have created: *There are two men, a woman, a baby and a car.*

Pupil 8 adds some more detail: *There were three people standing in a churchyard. There was a car.*

Pupil 9 is writing using more complexity and detail in their sentences. *It was a dark night when I came across a scene in the clearing of a churchyard. The moon was the only light and it glimmered, showing three people. Two were men, both wearing hats, the third, a woman, cradled a baby in her arms.* This pupil is developing a variety of literary skills through film that is captivating and engaging and evokes imagination.

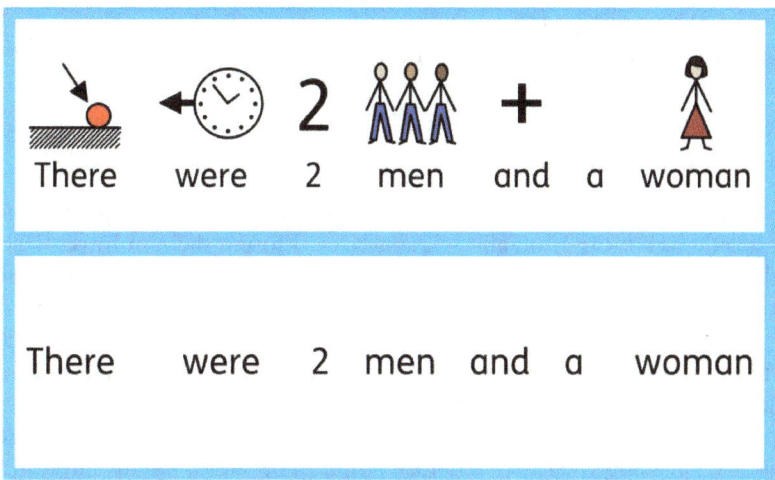

Figure 9.7 Telling the story with visual support
Source: © Widgit Software Ltd 2002–2024. www.widgit.com.

Figure 9.8 Sentence builder
Source: © Widgit Software Ltd 2002–2024. www.widgit.com.

Figure 9.9 Who is doing what
Source: © Widgit Software Ltd 2002–2024. www.widgit.com.

Comments

The lesson was a success as it included and engaged a range of pupils who at times could lack motivation and self-assurance. I found the film by researching on the internet and looking through films including those shared on Literacy Shed that would captivate the imagination of teenagers. The film was just over six minutes long and captured the pupils' attention throughout. The lack of surety of the details in *The Facts in the Case of Mister Hollow* enabled these same students to contribute and feel empowered in making their contributions. The muteness providing opportunity for the pupils to use their own voice to create a narrative, making their own interpretations. The music builds emotion and connection to the film and gives an alternative language to add to the plot. The mystery of the film allowed students to build on and express their own ideas and explore perception through their own and others' observations.

It is often difficult to find material that appeals to all, but film caters for these pupils well as it emphasises a multitude of possibilities and hooks pupils in for differing motives. It creates a learning environment around visual learning that promotes investigation and thought: this can reinforce learning at different levels without anyone feeling singled out. Film, visual literacy, and images are accessible to all. This specific film allows for young people to be challenged to think and to question, and to not rely on what they think they have seen. Employing such open and engaging films for exploration, pupils can realise their own ideas and feel confident in their voice, with teachers providing a positive space for pupils to realise a host of capabilities and possibilities.

Ideas for further activities

> **Questions**
>
> Create, answer, and record specific questions about what has been viewed, focusing on who, what, where, when, why, and how:
>
> Who is in the picture? Who do you think the characters are? What is happening in the pictures?
> Where was the picture taken? How do you think the characters got there? How do you know that the woman is frightened? Why do you think the characters are in the churchyard?
> Encourage the young people to make inferences and to work out the relationships and the possibilities implied in the film. The questions can vary and be differentiated to the abilities of the class. They could be open or closed questions or have multiple choices to refer to and pick from. The class could formulate and record their own questions. The rest of the class could reply using full sentences and reasons.

Descriptive writing

> Descriptive writing about some of the content in the photographs, for example, describe the initial scene set out in the photograph. Use adjectives to arouse mystery and add detail and interest to the descriptions. Learners who were working at an earlier stage of literacy development could talk about and pick out aspects of the photograph before labelling it with keywords. They could label parts of a still taken from the film individually, for example, the female character (label dress, hair, baby, eyes, etc.) or the man kneeling down (label hat, watch, match, fire, etc.)

Figure 9.10 A scene from *The Facts in the Case of Mister Hollow* to visualise the film

Source: © Permission from Someone at the Door Productions.

Crime reports

Create a crime report based on your observations and questions. Write the report as a newspaper report or as a police report. This could include writing witness statements. For some learners, the scaffolding could be higher and writing frames used. Alternatively, a cloze procedure method could be used for some learners to support them.

Character profiles

Create character profiles for each of the people represented in the photographs. Think about who they are. Describe them and write creatively about them. How did they end up at the scene? What is their story? This can be done again for a variety of levels of learning, developing word level based descriptions to more complex profiles which consider the background of the people depicted.

Write the film ending

How does it end? Consider in some detail what happened next.

Review

Write a film review. Use different levels of questions or leave open ended.

When choosing material for groups of learners, use a range of materials that optimally reflect a multicultural society that provides relatable positive images and role models. Find intriguing and inviting films that are thought provoking and appropriate for the intended audience.

Reference

Gudiño, R., & Marcone, V. (2008). *The facts in the case of Mr Hollow.* https://www.youtube.com/watch?v=bzw8qdXCep8

10 Using visuals and film to support literacy

Melanie Walker

When we think of literacy, we tend to think about reading books, writing stories, spelling, grammar, and punctuation. Although these areas are indeed imperative to language and communication, the way in which these skills are taught does not need to always be through the usual mediums that we tend to associate with literacy. I have found in my work with teenagers that linking literacy lessons with more functional skills such as those that might be used for interviews or in conversation with others. Writing a curriculum vitae (CV) or a personal report or even using emails or texts, for example, strengthens the importance to the learner and their motivation to learn and to do it well. Giving relevance and meaning to a task is crucial, and especially for those pupils who find learning more challenging.

The students I have taught have had an increased desire to improve their communicative independence in order to ascertain future employment opportunities and life skills. For this to be achieved, they must focus on developing their literary competence. One way of teaching the development of reading and comprehension skills, that I have found highly effective, is through script reading and role play. Learners develop confidence, comprehension skills, and communicative independence through mastering their understanding of the text. This links to the overall development of the skills mentioned previously. The pupils are invited to actively engage with others and develop social communication skills and literacy simultaneously, in a way that they feel that they have some mastery of.

In this chapter I outline an example of an inclusive literacy session with 12- to 14-year-olds with moderate learning disabilities. The chapter highlights the role and impact of active learning, using aspects of visual literacy to foster the engagement and participation of the class.

The lesson

Using visuals and film to support literacy works well on so many levels; the learners can illustrate their understanding of what they have read through inference and role play. Later, they are able to improve their performance, by reflecting on their learning through video recordings of their drama and script reading. We chose to study *The Hound of the Baskervilles* by Sir Arthur Conan Doyle as this tied in well with our detectives fictional stories theme.

DOI: 10.4324/9781003509141-10

Using visuals and film to support literacy 97

LESSON PLAN:	
THEME: Fictional Stories – Detectives Sherlock Holmes and The Hound of the Baskervilles	DATE:
	DURATION: 45 mins

LEARNING CHALLENGE

I will read and re-enact part of the script answering questions relating to the text to show that I understand what I have read

INTENDED PUPIL LEARNING OUTCOMES	ACTIVITIES	GROUPS
Group 1 – Read simplified version of the scripts and act out their chosen character's role; answer simple questions relating to the text to highlight understanding	Learners to be in smaller literacy groups. Teaching assistants to give a brief introduction to the play and what it's about. Learners to choose their characters and begin reading the first act of the script. Teaching assistants to ask questions relating to the text and gauge learner's comprehension (take videos for teacher assessment purposes). Learners to act out scene one and present to their peers. Learners to rate their learning **Extension tasks** Can you predict what might happen next? Write/act out and record you prediction. Why do you think this will happen?	Group 1 **Teaching Assistant** – Lizzy **Learners** – Mia, Owen, Craig, Sally
Group 2 – Read a less simplified version of the script and act out the roles of their chosen characters; answer questions relating to the text to highlight understanding		Group 2 **Teaching Assistant** – Debbie **Learners** – Ben, Mohammed, Aman, Hana
Group 3 – Read the full script and act out the roles of their chosen characters and answer more complex questions relating to the text to highlight understanding		Group 3 **Teaching Assistant** – Branka **Learners** – Molly, Aysha, Jasmine, Shane, Steve

ASSESSMENT PLAN

Achievement of learning objectives will be assessed throughout the session by observation, video recording, and after the session feedback from class team (teachers and teaching assistants). Use reward chart for good effort/behaviour.

98 *Positive Special Education*

Key areas for consideration are as follows:
- Application of understanding
- Individual literacy targets
- Evidence of independent skills
- Evidence of effective communication and comprehension (speaking/listening)

STRATEGIES (including timing)	Teacher input/questions/explanations/Pupil activities/resources/organisation
Introduction 10 minutes	Class teacher to introduce the Play (*Hound of the Baskervilles*) – showing picture of the front cover of the playscript and asking what learners think the play might be about. Give brief description of story and setting. Using pictures on the interactive white board to support understanding and predictive skills
Main Activity 25 minutes Vocabulary/Show understanding/speaking and listening skills	Teacher input/questions/explanations/resources; Pupil activities/resources/organisation Group 1 – Guided reading of Act 1 in the simplified scripts. Adults to assist learners in their reading where necessary. Once the learners have finished the co-reading, check for understanding by sequencing the story using the pictures from the script. 　The learners will choose a character to play and as a group perform the first act. Adult to record and review later. 　Check for understanding – Questions 1. Who are the characters in the play? 2. What has happened first, second, third? SUCCESS CRITERIA Comprehension through sequencing, drama, and questioning. - Can I sequence the story? Have I understood the story/plot? - Can I tell you which picture came first/second/third? - Have I been able to match the sentences/symbols to the correct picture? Group 2 – Learners and adults to choose their characters. Learners to follow the scrips and identify their character's lines as independently as possible. Check for understanding – Questions 1. Who is Sherlock Holmes? 2. Who is John Watson? 3. What is their job? 4. Where is the story set? Act out their parts taking turns to record their performance.

Using visuals and film to support literacy 99

		SUCCESS CRITERIA **Comprehension through drama and questioning.** • Have I understood the story/plot so far? • Can I answer questions with a degree of accuracy relating to the text/story? • Can I briefly explain what might happen next? Group 3 – Learners and adults to choose their characters. Learners to follow the scrips and identify their character's lines independently. Check for understanding – Questions 1. What do you think about Sherlock Holmes as a character? How would you describe him? 2. What do you think John Watson's relationship with Sherlock is like? 3. Do you think they are a good team? Why? 4. How would you describe the setting? Why do you think the writer chose to set the story there? Act out their parts taking turns to record their performance **SUCCESS CRITERIA** **Comprehension through drama and questioning.** • Have I understood the story/plot so far? Can I relay this back to a friend? • Can I make inferences about the characters and the plot? • Do I have an understanding of the way the writer creates atmosphere? • Can I make an informed prediction on what may happen next?
Plenary/ Conclusion *10 minutes*		Teacher input/questions/explanations/resources; Pupil activities/resources/organisation • Class to share recording of the first act performance, discuss the story so far, the characters' actions, feelings, and share predictions for the next act.
RESOURCES		Script/pictures/symbols/sentences/iPod/iPad/interactive white board

Above is an example of a lesson plan that effectively includes all the learners through drama, video, and script writing and outlines the aims of the lesson, the assessment possibilities, and the structure of the lesson itself.

Learning outcomes

When teaching a group of learners with moderate learning difficulties, it is usually necessary to differentiate for at least three separate groups, to pitch the lesson correctly for all students and engage them in the learning successfully. The task needs to be challenging enough for the learner, without being frustrating and potentially demotivating. This includes the level at which the work is set as well as the questioning.

The higher-level questioning for a group of learners for example will include more complicated, in-depth questions relating to more complex text. In this instance I would ask the learners to make inferences, predictions, and give more elaborate descriptions of the characters. I would then adapt the level of the text or script to make it challenging yet accessible for the lower groups and ask more basic questions relating to their comprehension of the plot/story and characters.

The simplified example in the next section shows how the meaning of the text is kept but is presented in a different way to ensure meaning is not lost and aid pupils' understanding. The students will later use the pictures to aid sequencing the first act in the play.

Groups 2 and 3 will read directly from the script.

For all learners, but particularly those with SEND, it is important to ensure that pupils are actively involved in their learning and that they learn to understand and comprehend what they are reading and not simply decode the letters and words they perceive. There is a lot of information available to them in their daily lives; on social media, newspapers, advertisements, television, magazines, and the internet. Learners need to be able to take this information in and make sense of it for them to navigate their day to day. Learning comprehension skills actively and through drama brings the text to life and enables pupils to interact with it, using visual stimuli to support pupil engagement and participation in a way that they find fun, relevant, and interesting, as well as having the additional benefits on negotiating speaking and listening with others. The use of role play is a great way to assess pupil understanding through the ways that the pupils interpret the character's demeanour, actions, thoughts, and feelings. The use of questioning as assessment prompts is important at this stage to gain a clear understanding (see questioning prompts on planning example in the previous section). Once we had completed each act, we would then watch the act in the film adaptation of *The Hound of the Baskervilles*. This complemented the script and role plays perfectly, as we discussed in our groups the similarities and differences between them. We were also able to build on this by communicating our thoughts and preferences between the script and film.

Using visuals and film to support literacy 101

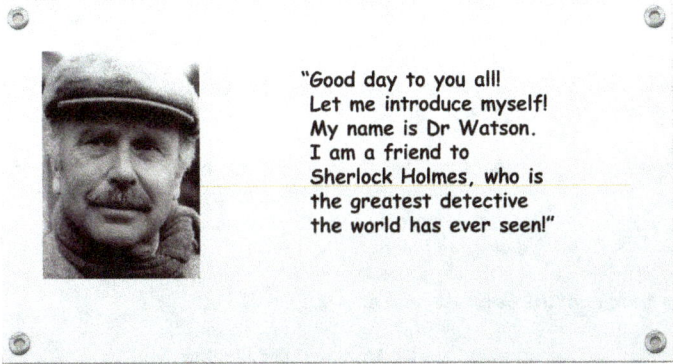

Figure 10.1 Dr. Watson introduces himself

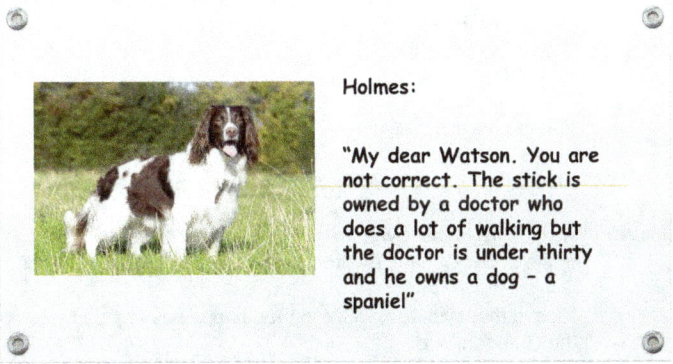

Figure 10.2 Holmes comments to Dr. Watson

This lends itself to further class discussions regarding the period and modern adaptations of the film. We drew comparisons and discussed the atmosphere and settings within each film. Some learners chose to record a video blog, or vlog, reviewing their chosen adaptation of the film; other learners chose to write a review or character profile. By watching back their own video entries, pupils have opportunities for further self-reflection, and this can be used to develop more traditional areas of literacy including sentence structure, etc., but also develop those more subtle communication skills, such as body language, eye contact, and facial expressions.

There are endless learning opportunities that come from film studies and visual prompts to promote critical thinking and develop literacy skills. Having only selected a few, I hope you find it useful and are able to build your own ideas and teaching into developing the language and communication through film and visuals in your own classroom.

Scene 1

🔊 TRACK 1

(A large living room in Baskerville Hall, a manor house located in the English mountains. Dr. Mortimer is on stage reading a diary.)

DR. MORTIMER: *(Reading.)* "March, 27th 1892. Of the origin of the hound of the Baskervilles there have been many statements. Hugo Baskerville was murdered by a big black beast. It was the biggest hound I had ever seen before."

(Someone knocks at the door. Watson enters.)

WATSON: Oh there you are Dr. Mortimer! Did I frighten you?

DR. MORTIMER: Oh no! You'll never know how grateful I am that you are here, Watson! Where is Mr. Holmes?

WATSON: He will be here soon. *(Looking at his watch)* in five ... four .... three ... two ... (**Holmes enters.**)

HOLMES: And one!

WATSON: You are always on time!

HOLMES: Elementary my dear Watson.

DR. MORTIMER: A pleasure to meet you Mr. Holmes. I'm Dr. Mortimer. I was a very close friend of Sir. Charles Baskerville; he used to be the owner of this house.

HOLMES: Nice to meet you too, Dr. Mortimer. I hope you enjoyed your walk around the Grimpen Mire.

DR. MORTIMER: How do you know I have been there?

HOLMES: Because I can see some mud on your shoes. And that kind of mud is only found there.

The differentiation can be done individually, or within a larger class: the key point is that whoever is in the class in front of you, regardless of their stage of development, it is possible to personalise the learning inclusively: our aim as effective educators is to be able to think about all of the pupils in the class and to find a way to tailor our planning for all, through self-reflection on video coverage.

11 Positive special education

Challenge students to read and write in a creative way without fixed material

Ann-Katrin Swärd

In this chapter I will give a picture how funny and fruitful it can be both for students in need of extra support, as those learning without any difficulties, and their teacher to teach in a systematic and structured way how to read and write. The working methods described in the chapter are suitable to reach all students' learning ability. There are different ways of working, different reading methods or reading models that in different ways support and stimulate students' reading and writing. The model from which this text partly based is the Witting method because teachers who work with it do not use ready-made material, but the students create their own.

First, the letter sounds (phoneme) must be mastered regardless of method

In most reading models and ready-made reading material, reading instruction begins with the most frequent sounds and letters in the Swedish language. It can always be difficult to find the perfect reading material, which places demands on the teachers' competence about the reading process as well as on their ability to critically examine different materials purely in terms of content. Above all, it can be difficult to find material that contains the words that the students already know and have experience of. Not least if the students have a different mother tongue. Taking advantage of the students' own words and working from them is an important starting point in the Witting method (Swärd, 2008).

Important to be linguistically aware

When the children begin compulsory school, it is important that the teacher gets to know each student's linguistic development. There are students who need a lot of support from the start, while others have already learned to read. When students have more extensive difficulties in learning to read and write, it becomes even more important that the teacher works with well-adapted activities that are fully understandable to the student. Through this, the student also receives support in developing their metacognitive ability and being a co-assessor of their own learning as well as the teacher's teaching (ibid.).

There is broad agreement among reading researchers that when students understand that letters and sounds can be read and written, it means that they have reached an important level of linguistic awareness. Reading contains several aspects, such as being phonologically aware, having knowledge of the written language, being able to decode quickly, having an expanded vocabulary, and understanding what the writing wants to convey (Chall, 1967; Stanovich & Stanovich, 1995; Adams, 2001; Myrberg, 2003).

Over the years as a special education teacher, I have many times wished that all children could experience reading aloud from the first day of life, but it was not and still is not that simple. Many are the children who grow up without being able to experience different texts through reading aloud or oral stories. The digital world tends to take over more of this, which is important to be aware of because the story on an iPad can never replace the human proximity and voice. The home, the preschool, and then the school have an important task by creating these reading environments for all children and students, regardless of age.

In a study done by me and a school librarian in Värnamo, there were some boys in middle school who never read. They claimed that there were no fun or interesting books in the entire library. It is important that teachers identify boys' different areas of interest to find books that also appeal to boys who, for various reasons, do not read. During the time the project was ongoing, several boys increased their interest in reading (Karlsson & Swärd, 2014).

Independent work and taking responsibility for one's learning

According to Witting (1985) and Swärd (2008), an important start in the method is that students learn to work independently, which means taking responsibility for the task. The way of working means that the students become aware of what they can do, what they have not yet learned, and what it means to work independently or cooperate in a group and help each other.

Students learn best when the language activities are fun and, above all, clear. The variation in the teaching is best if there is a structure and a clarity and a system in how the students should tackle the different tasks (Swärd, 2008). The independent work that the Witting method describes is not only important for taking responsibility for one's own learning. It also means that students can continue to work on different activities when the teacher is busy helping other students.

When the students start the class, the teacher asks what the students like to do. The students then have different suggestions, such as painting, drawing, writing, doing puzzles, reading, etc., depending on what they have already learned. Based on the different answers that the students give, the teacher makes sure that there is access to different materials in the classroom (Witting, 1985; Swärd, 2008).

Collaboration in creative work

When the students have learned all letter sounds (phonemes) and mastered writing them (graphemes), it immediately becomes both fun and more motivating to work on their own reading and writing development. In the Witting method, this is done by having students listen to combinations of vowels and consonants (content-neutral language structures), say them out loud, and then write them down. By both listening, remembering which phonemes are part of the structure, pronouncing these, and then writing them down, the student gets memory support. It is an individual activity, but when the students have done this, creative work begins (Swärd, 2008) by working in pairs or small groups, collective learning. They share each other's words, create sentences, stories, fairy tales, songs, and poems. By working together and having completely free hands to create different types of texts, the students become motivated. They also learn the important role of phonemes in writing and reading and then move on to more difficult written language tasks. The students also create their own pictures that symbolise in different ways what they want to talk about. The working method rests on positive special education about all students' opportunities for development and learning and that learning is best done through collaboration.

In the Witting method, the reading consists of two parts. The first is the symbol function, the same as being able to decode, that is, using language sounds (phonemes) and signs (graphemes). This part of the reading must be overlearned for the reading to become automatic. This is done by the students practicing this. The second part is understanding, understanding the meaning of all words and what the text wants to convey.

Understanding cannot be overlearned because new texts with new words need to be worked on. For students who have an automated symbol function, it means a basis for understanding new words and texts (Witting, 1985; Swärd, 2008).

Reading comprehension is a must in all methods

In a democracy, all citizens should be able to make their voice heard, be able to participate in general elections, and be involved in different ways as further elaborated in the chapter by Monica Reichenberg (2024). This assumes that the information is clear and written in an understandable way, but at the same time the individual must understand what is to be read. Students who have an intellectual disability often find it more difficult to understand the written language even if they have cracked the code.

Lundberg and Reichenberg (2013) show in their intervention study that reading comprehension increased in students with intellectual disability in adapted elementary schools when the teachers worked consciously on this. In other words, there is evidence that different working methods support students to increase their reading comprehension. The students need to be able to process these words and concepts in different ways to understand and be able to use them in adequate situations. By having the teacher and students talk about the texts used, the conditions for understanding increase, not only of words and concepts but of the entire context (Reichenberg, 2014). When students speak, draw, communicate without spoken language, or write, it is important for those who are to receive the information that the words chosen are correct in the context in which they are used. In her research, Pickl (2008) has shown how important it is that the school uses different aids and alternative communication when the students lack verbal language.

Students whose mother tongue is different naturally also need to be able to work with the words and their meaning, which can be done through oral narration according to Henricsson and Lundgren (2016). When Matt Maguire in his chapter (2024) describes and develop how he and the students work with functional reading, it becomes even more clear how important it is for students to interpret and understand the images and words around them, in school and in society.

The writing is there from the beginning

Just like the interest in reading, the interest in writing is also affected by the environment the child grows up in. In environments where writing occurs, even the small child begins to write in his own way. It is the beginning of continued writing which, as the child learns more, becomes more grammatically correct. The students need to be given the opportunity to prepare what they want to write about. The words must turn into sentences and turn into a text, which others must read and be able to understand.

From my own experiences, writing, for some students, feels like a high wall to climb over, and they find it difficult to motivate themselves to write. Perhaps the student has not yet learned to write fully or have difficulties of various kinds. According to Fitzgerald and Shanahan (2000) students get more ideas to write about the more experience and knowledge they have about different topics and everyday things. Just as with reading, the student needs to feel meaningful to be motivated to want to write. Since writing is important for the student to develop language and thinking, it is important that all teachers teach about writing in different contexts (Lundberg, 2008).

The different dimensions of writing

Regardless of the pedagogical direction the teacher chooses, the students should get to create texts and work with different kinds of texts. There is a difference between writing an argumentative text and a fiction text, and students must learn this. When students have different degrees or types of difficulties, it may be enough for them to only be able to somehow write how they feel and what they want, tell something, or just write a greeting (Swärd & Karlsson, 2017).

Sometimes the discussion arises about which writing implements should be used. I can consider this to some extent a non-issue because it is important to choose a tool that suits the student's needs. If the student has difficulty using a pen, it is pointless to practise this when we now have many different digital options. If students can, it is of course good to learn to use both pencil and digital options. There are no studies that have investigated whether one is better than the other. For some students, eye control via the computer is the only option, while other students may be able to choose between different options depending on the purpose of the activity. However, what may be more important to discuss and reflect on is how a text is created. What does the student need to know to produce a readable text?

Various teaching activities create opportunities for all students

The didactic, such as subject content together with the teachers' pedagogical competence, becomes important for the teacher's confidence in his own ability to teach as well as for the student's opportunity to succeed in his learning, to increase his own confidence.

Based on the variety of students that teachers meet; it is important to understand that everyone comes to school with different images of what they should learn and how learning takes place. In addition, the students have different family backgrounds and may have different mother tongues, which places demands on the teachers to create a learning environment that meets the different needs of all students (Kansanen, 2000). One of my students had some difficulties with written language and often use spoken word when writing:

> That I "shod" do, wrote one student. I asked what "shod" mean even if I could guess what. This student was in grade 3 and we discussed why this word should (in Swedish – skulle) spell should and not "shod" (in Swedish – sulle) in written language. Home we only say "shod", said the student. Sure, I answered but that is when talking – now you are going to write a text.

We discussed the difference between talking and writing and why there are rules in the written language that help all of us to understand what we read. Otherwise, it could be interesting and creative if all students could spell and write from words in their different dialects, but it is not that easy.

Students are different, come from different background environments, and may need support in developing linguistic awareness (Stadler, 1998). Children learn language by using it. For some children, language development looks different, and they need different support. Through many years of studies of children with different linguistic and intellectual development, Johansson (1996) has studied which type of activities best favour their linguistic development. Factors that proved to give positive results included clear structure, especially individually adapted material and method and perhaps primarily regular and frequently occurring language activities. Johansson's (1996)[1] results about a clear structure and systematic way of working also apply to other teaching, regardless of the students' needs.

The importance of teaching

The sense of coherence, KASAM (Antonovsky, 1991), can be an important foundation to work from. Everything that each student must do must be comprehensible; the student must therefore understand what he must do. In addition, the student must be able to perform the work with or without support, that is, the work must be manageable. That something is comprehensible and manageable means that it is experienced as meaningful, and meaningfulness and motivation are an important part of learning.

Through classroom-based research, Hugo (2007) showed that meaningfulness was of great importance for students to be motivated to come to school. A close relationship with the teacher was an important factor, and students needed to be affirmed as people and not just as students. It was also important that the students were allowed to participate and felt that they were involved in deciding the content and form of the teaching. Hugo's results show that motivation must come from within the student. In the beginning it may work with external rewards, but after a while it becomes irrelevant. The student must come to the inner feeling that things are going well, that "it's fun when I'm me". When the student gets there through the response the teacher gives, both self-esteem and self-confidence increase, and above all, a belief in one's own ability is created.

Teaching also means assessing and evaluating

During my first years as a teacher in special education, I worked with various subjects and subject areas at one adapted elementary school. There was not much material, especially not for students studying subject areas. Over the years, more and more material came, but before that, many of us teacher produced our own material. The students' learning should be put in relation to the teaching and competence that the teacher has. If the student does not learn or develop in different areas, it can be assumed that the teaching is not adapted to that student.

Although I have never worked with the Witting method, but only researched it, I realise that the method has great benefits when it comes to reviewing progress and teaching together with the student. In this method, the student becomes a co-assessor of the activities planned by the teacher. Through discussion, collaboration, and positive feedback, the student learns to assess what he can handle and what needs to be learned (Witting, 2003). When a student in my study turns out to only have three vowels and seven consonants for sure, the student is surprised but at the same time understands why nine years in elementary school put him in many subjects and why it has always struggled to tackle reading.

Different working methods and their importance

In a longitudinal study, Tang et al., (2019) investigated the connection between teachers' different working methods and reading development from grade 1 to grade 3. Using the ECCOM, a standardised observation instrument (Early

Childhood Classroom Observation Measure), 32 teachers were observed in grade 1. The number of students was 359, and the instrument was adapted to word recognition and sentence reading for students in grades 1–3. In the analysis of the collected data, three different teaching practices were identified: (1) child-oriented teaching, (2) teacher-oriented teaching, and (3) a mixture of these two. The students whose teachers used the mixed method showed faster reading development than the students whose teachers used only the teacher-oriented method.

The result was thus that if teachers use a mixture of child- and teacher-oriented methods during the first school years, it gives the best reading and writing development, which also lasts over time. Through this way of working, the teachers offer varied teaching that involves shared responsibility between teachers and students. Although the study is small with only 32 teachers, the researchers believe that it is one of the few studies that shows the importance of didactics and constructivist practice complementing each other and can be used effectively (Tang et al., 2019). Shared responsibility between teacher and student fits well with the way of working advocated by the Witting method.

Prevention is always better than repair

Most people probably agree that prevention of difficulties is the best. Although it is never too late to learn, many failures have affected one's confidence and self-esteem. Regardless of whether it is about adults who never had the opportunity to learn to read and write or whether it is people who have an intellectual disability, it is of course possible to learn later in life (Wramner, 2020). Swärd and Florin (2014) also highlight the importance of planning and teacher competence for student's learning. In addition, they problematise the importance of teachers, students, and guardians working together.

For this tripartite collaboration to work, it is necessary that the teachers create trust and get involved in everything that has to do with the individual student. When this happens, preventive work can be seen as an ongoing process during the student's entire time at school. With this positive special education approach, the requirements of the task are adapted so that the student can cope with it with or without support. It is therefore necessary to meet the student's current competence. Every time the student succeeds, difficulties and failures are prevented which will be further developed in the chapter by Anna-Carin Jonsson (2024). In addition, the student feels better, can maintain his self-esteem, his self-confidence, and finally, his belief in his own ability to learn.

Summary

In this chapter I have highlighted various aspects of reading and writing and the complexity of these areas. The common denominator for all parts concerns the teacher's way of teaching and the choice of method and materials, as well as the importance of motivation. It is about how the teaching can be made more creative in different ways to reach the students' interests. It is always easier if the students find it fun, if the motivation is there when they must learn things. It is easy to say and write that teaching should be creative and fun, but not always so easy to achieve in everyday work. For most students, things are going well, even if they have had to struggle for a while. For some students, the struggle never ends, and then it can be even more difficult to find motivation and meaning in what is to be learned.

There are many ways for teachers to work with reading and writing instruction. The important thing that I tried to describe is the competence the teacher has about how the actual reading and writing process takes place. The Witting method is the model I used as an example, and I have done so because that model has a clear structure and a systematic way of working. In addition, the teachers who have chosen to work with that model have had the opportunity for continuous training.

An important aspect of the model is the continuous documentation and follow-up that each teacher has. This security check means that the teachers make sure that all students can succeed. If they discover someone who is having a difficulty, they take care of this immediately. In addition, there are several fun activities that increase the motivation of the students. From all the words that students create based on content-neutral language structures, they can create texts of various kinds. The texts can be poems, songs, rap songs, and much more. That's how it should be in all methods.

I want to end this chapter by reflecting about how many students must struggle all their schooltime and still as adults need to do so, which shows even more clearly how important different forms of support are. Without good and relevant support at the right level and with a home environment that offered no hope, students' development might look different. When students with learning disabilities succeed, it gives hope to other to struggle, even if learning to read and write can be extremely tough at times, because everything is possible when students have great faith in their own ability.

Acknowledgements

This chapter was originally published in Sweden (2020) in the book *Positiv Specialpedagogik. Teorier och tillämpningar*. To meet the new requirements for publishing in English, some adjustments have been done. To meet international readers, the English chapter has been fully revised.

Note

1 Johansson created Karlstadmodellen, a reading model for students with intellectual disabilities.

References

Adams, M. J. (2001). *Beginning to read, thinking and learning about print*. MIT Press.
Antonovsky, A. (1991). *Hälsans mysterium*. Natur & Kultur.
Chall, J. S. (1967). *Learning to read: The great debate*. McGraw-Hill.

Fitzgerald, J., & Shanahan, T. (2000). Reading and writing relations and their development. *Educational Psychologist, 35,* 39–50.
Henricsson, O., & Lundgren, M. (2016). *Muntligt berättande i flerspråkiga klassrum.* Studentlitteratur.
Hugo, M. (2007). *Liv och lärande i gymnasieskolan: En studie om elevers och lärares erfarenheter i en liten grupp på gymnasieskolans individuella program.* Diss. Högskolan i Jönköping.
Johansson, I. (1996). *Språkutveckling hos handikappade barn 3 Enkel grammatik.* Studentlitteratur.
Jonsson, A.-C. (2024). Special educational consequences of implicit notions of ability. In M. Reichenberg, A.-K. Swärd & C. Shipton (Eds.), *Positive special education: Theories, applications and inspiration* (pp. 23–31). Routledge.
Kansanen, P. (2000). Kampen mellan vetenskap och lära. In E. Alerby, P. Kansanen & T. Kroksmark (Red.), *Lära om lärande* (pp. 29–44). Studentlitteratur.
Karlsson, A., & Swärd, A.-K. (2014). *Pojkar läser – ett läsprojekt i Värnamo kommun.* Pojkar läser. http://pojkarlaservarnamo.blogspot.se/
Lundberg, I. (2008). *God skrivutveckling-kartläggning och undervisning.* Natur & Kultur.
Lundberg, I., & Reichenberg, M. (2013). Developing reading comprehension among students with mild intellectual disabilities: An intervention study. *Scandinavian Journal of Educational Research, 57*(1), 89–100.
Maquire, M. (2024). Teaching functional literacy to pupils with SEN. In M. Reichenberg, A.-K. Swärd & C. Shipton (Eds.), *Positive special education: Theories, applications and inspiration* (pp. 70–76). Routledge.
Myrberg, M. (2003). *Att skapa konsensus om skolans insatser för att motverka läs- och skrivsvårigheter.* Rapport Från "Konsensus-Projektet.
Pickl, G. (2008). *Children with complex communication needs. The parents' perspective.* Diss. Stockholms Universitet.
Reichenberg, M. (2014). *Vägar till läsförståelse: Texten, läsaren, samtalet.* Natur & Kultur.
Reichenberg, M. (2024). Positive special education: Why are teachers' and students' self-efficacy important? Consequences for reading instruction and civic education. In M. Reichenberg, A.-K. Swärd & C. Shipton (Eds.), *Positive special education: Theories, applications and inspiration* (pp. 7–22). Routledge.
Stadler, E. (1998). *Läs- och skrivinlärning.* Studentlitteratur.
Stanovich, K. E. & Stanovich, P. J. (1995). How research might inform the debate about early reading acquisition. *Journal of Research in Reading, 18,* 87–105.
Swärd, A.-K. (2008). *Att säkerställa skriftspråklighet genom medveten arrangering. Wittingmetodens tillämpning i några olika lärandemiljöer.* Doktorsavhandling. Stockholms universitet.
Swärd, A.-K., & Florin, K. (2014). *Särskolans verksamhet: Uppdrag, pedagogik och bemötande.* Studentlitteratur.
Swärd, A.-K., & Karlsson, A. (2017). *Ett skrivutvecklande arbetssätt. Att skriva med lust och glädje.* Studentlitteratur.
Tang, X., Pakarinen, E., Lerkkanen, M.-K., Muotka, J., & Nurmi, J.-E. (2019). Longitudinal associations of first-grade teaching with reading in early primary school. *Journal of Applied Developmental Psychology, 63,* 23–32.
Witting, M. (1985). *Metod för läs- och skrivinlärning.* Ekelunds förlag.
Witting, M. (2003). *Att kritiskt granska sin egen undervisning: Kontinuerlig undervisningsanalys – viktigt led i en metodutveckling och möjlig form för en metodfortbildning.* Ekelunds förlag.
Wramner, L. (2020). Blodanalysen var normal – det kunde jag läsa alldeles själv. In A.-K. Swärd, M. Reichenberg & S. Fischbein (Eds.), *Positiv specialpedagogik Teorier och tillämpningar.* Studentlitteratur.

12 Learning words and understanding their morphological structures

Solveig-Alma Halaas Lyster

This chapter focuses on the important role vocabulary knowledge plays in reading comprehension. It focuses on the form and content of words and on how words are composed of morphemes, the smallest elements in words that carry meaning. More specifically, it discusses how children with different kinds of reading challenges can be supported in developing an understanding of how words are built by morphemes. Helping students to develop morphological awareness provides a kind of "morphological tool" to understand new words and hence, may support students' self-efficacy, with confidence in their ability to learn new words and to understand what they read. Self-efficacy is important for learning and development and will be more elaborated in the chapter by Monica Reichenberg (2024).

Students with a learning disability, and especially students with an intellectual disability, meet many challenges in school (Lyster et al., 2021).

Children with language disabilities know fewer words than their peers, and the quality of their word knowledge is poor (McGregor et al., 2013).

Particular difficulties are faced by many students with Down syndrome who have restricted vocabulary (Laws et al., 2016; Næss et al., 2012). Language teaching is therefore very important for these groups of students and, as I shall argue, training morphological skills can have a positive impact on students' vocabulary and reading development. It varies much what focus morphological structures of words have been given in working with students' language and reading development. Therefore, I will first present how different morphemes add meanings to root words. Then I will present some evidence for the effect of morphological knowledge on language development and reading comprehension. The last part of this paper will focus on words and morphemes to choose and on activities that have been found effective in developing morphological awareness.

Why morphemes?

Morphological structure

When considering morphological structure, it is important to differentiate "free" from "bound" morphemes. Root morphemes are free morphemes, which means they can stand alone, and they can also be combined to make compound words. The word "dog", for example, may give the main meaning to compound words like "watchdog" and "sheepdog". The same word may also be the first part in the compound word "doghouse", describing the kind of house "doghouse" is.

Prefixes such as *un-* in "untidy" and suffixes such as *-ing* in "walk*ing*" are examples of bound morphemes. Bound morphemes have no meaning on their own, but when combined with a word, they alter its meaning. Notwithstanding this, some bound morphemes are identical in form to a root morpheme, for example, *-less* in "need*less*" and *in-* in "*in*dependent". Some words have only one root morpheme, but adding bound morphemes can change its meaning. Inflectional morphemes change the grammatical form of a word. For example, adding the inflectional morpheme *-s* to the noun "car" changes it into the plural form "cars", whereas adding inflections to a verb changes the tense or aspect, for example, "walk" -> "walks", "walked" or "walking". The suffix *-ed* in the regular verb "jump*ed*" tells us that this action has taken place; it is something that has happened. If Peter walks the dog, however, that is something going on at the moment or something he does every day.

Grammatical morphemes can also be added to adverbs and adjectives. "Hard", as in "Peter works hard", can be compared with "hard*er*" and "hard*est*", changing the way Peter works, and "young" can be changed to "young*er*" and "youngest". In some words the phonological structure of a root morpheme changes when bound morphemes are added, for example, "sign" changes to "signal". The root morpheme keeps its orthographic structure, a discovery that has been shown to support spelling skills (Bourassa & Treiman, 2008).

A further type of morpheme is derivational. Derivational morphemes alter the syntactic class of both nouns and verbs, and adding a derivational morpheme to a word result in a new lexical item. Thus, for nouns, adding "dom" (as in *domicile* or *domestic*) to "king" -> "kingdom" and adding "ist" to "guitar" -> "guitarist". For verbs "sing" -> "singer", and "read" -> "readable"; friend can change to the plural form friends, but other affixes change the syntactic class: friend*less*, friend*ship*, *un*friend*ly* etc.

Knowing that *un-* in front of "finished" gives a word with an opposite meaning, may help children to understand words like "unskilled", "ungraceful", and "unfriendly". In addition, knowing that the prefix *anti-* means "against" or "the opposite of" can help students understand words like "anti-climax", "antiseptic", "antibody", etc.

A study by Hiebert et al., (2018) show clearly that most of the words in texts across the school years can be parsed into a relatively small number of morphological families. This is also true of children's literature: in a popular Swedish children's book, Pippi *Longstocking*, for example, there are many derived words such as "unfortunately", "astonishment", "disappointed", and "speechless", and compound words, such as "longtailed", "playmate" and, "woodbox". Pippi also creates her own compound words which, while nonsense, are filled with meaning. Pippi calls herself a "thing-finder" and a "turnupstuffer" meaning that she collects stuff or things that turn up! And Pippi is strong, yes, but not only strong*er* than Tommy and Anniken, she is the "strong*est* girl in the world".

Importantly, then, children meet a huge range of compound words and derivations through the books they read and are read to them before they go to school. They understand that verbs give information about when an action takes or took place and that adjectives and adverbs can indicate comparisons. Some children discover the systematic ways words are built by themselves; others need support to discover the patterns in words and the meaning of the morphemes that build a word.

Morphological skills and reading development

In a Norwegian study I showed that morphological awareness training in preschool (when children were between 5 and 6 years) was effective and influenced later reading development (Lyster, 2002), with a long-term impact on reading comprehension some 6 years later (Lyster et al., 2016). The intervention in this study comprised a number of components: (i) children were taught how words could combine to make compound words and that the last word in such a compound word carried the main meaning of the word; (ii) they identified single words in compounds and figured out what happened to the main meaning if two words in a compound changed places (basketball/ballbasket); (iii) they examined differences between words with or without affixes, for example, happy and unhappy, boy and boys, walked and walking. These exercises were embedded in playful activities adapted to the children's age and in a way that helped them be aware of grammatical morphemes, prefixes and suffixes. Further, different forms of adjectives and adverbs were presented, and the children learned to listen to the endings that could be added. The word "quick", for example, could have the ending *-er* and *-est*: Peter was quick walking on his way to school, but Anna was quick*er* – she used her bike. John was quick*est*, though, since he was driven by his father. In this way, the children learned how these suffixes added some new information to the words in focus. The children enjoyed working with words this way, and it was always possible to give support in a way that gave all of them a feeling of success.

All words, roots and roots with the different additional morphemes, were presented in different contexts, and some words were presented in written forms even if the group of children did not yet learn to read. We used flannel boards; large, flat screens covered with flannel to which we could attach any picture or piece of paper with some flannel or sandpaper on the back. The teachers would for example present the word "car" in spoken and written form together with a drawing and then ask, "What do we say if we have more than one car?" (In Norwegian bil + er = biler). The children would be asked about the difference they could hear between

Figure 12.1 Identify letter *s* and use it

car/cars. When the sound /s/ was identified, the letter *s* would be added to the word "car" on the flannel board, and above the word two or more cars were presented.

There are several morphological awareness training programmes developed for students.

For some students, however, "homemade" material like in Figure 12.1 might be both more interesting to use and give more ownership to the activities than using the more sophisticated material developed for iPads and electronic blackboards.

Similarly, together with Brinchmann and Hjetland I have shown that teaching poor readers in Grades 3 and 4 about word structure (both phonological and morphological) supports their vocabulary development as well as their reading (Brinchmann et al., 2016). The words chosen in this study were so-called academic words that could be found in school texts; they were spoken, read in a text, and written. The structure of the chosen words and the meaning of the morphological parts were discussed with the students. In this study we composed texts that were connected to themes that were on the agenda for different subjects, for example pollution. Words important to the theme were explained and discussed. In addition, we included words with prefixes and suffixes that would be found in many of the texts used in the classroom. An example from one of the texts is given here.

Pollution

We have to take care of the world we live in. We have to take care of the birds and the animals and the fish in the sea. *Wildlife* in Africa is threatened by snipers, and the air we breathe are in many places very polluted. *Marine* life suffers from a huge waste of plastic and from *overfishing*.

Pollution can be explained by throwing or placing *harmful* stuff into the environment. For a long time we have been *unaware* of how threatened our world is by pollution. We have to *rethink* how we can save the earth and our future, and we have to *undo* the way we live our lives.

What can we do? Can we go *paperless* to save the *rainforest*? What more can we do to stop plastic from being produced?

In addition to the words "pollution" and "marine" there is a range of compound words, prefixes, and suffixes that could be focused in this text. Some of the morphemes, however, are just repeated from earlier lessons and texts, and "new" morphemes such as *-ful* as in "harmful", *-less* as in "paperless", and *re-* as in "rethink" were the main morphemes of the week when this text was used. In addition to being guided to discover the meaning of the morphemes in question, the students were hunting for other words with the same morphemes, for example words ending with *-less*: "colourless", "homeless", "sleepless", "helpless", "useless", etc. Repeated reading also took place; repeated reading of words and repeated reading of texts to ensure access to the orthographic structure of words was automatic (Lee & Yoon, 2017). The programme was found to benefit both word comprehension and reading.

In the following paragraphs more ideas about words and morphemes to choose and ways to set up lessons will be given. The main idea is not to just explain a word's meaning to the students but to discuss word structure and word and morpheme meaning *with* the students.

Setting up an intervention programme

What words to introduce

While many prefixes and suffixes can be trained from the early grades, students also benefit from learning words connected to different subjects – the so-called "academic" vocabulary they will meet. Words like "argue", "additional", "purpose", as well as "mislead", "overcharge", and "cooperate" can be counted as "academic words". The student's linguistic level and the textbooks they work with will decide what words and affixes to teach. The prefix *un-* can be used in front of happy in preschool and grade 1, while a word like *un*predict*able* probably will be a better fit in grade 5.

Table 12.1 shows how teachers can prepare lists of prefixes and words that students might meet in texts they will be reading, and Latin and Greek prefixes

Table 12.1 Examples of some common prefixes

Prefix	Meaning	Examples
re-	again	repeat, reheat, revisit
un-	Not	unsafe, unhappy, undo
pre-	Before	Preview, predict, prejudice
dis-	not, none	disappear, disagree, disentangle
mis-	wrong, bad	misadventure, misunderstand, mistake
mini-	small, little	miniskirt, minibus, minimum
anti-	against, opposite of	anticlimax, antiaircraft, antiseptic
over-	too much, above	overcrowded, overpriced, overacting
hyper-	over, more than usual, beyond	hyperactive, hypersensitive, hypercritical
mono-	One	monologue, monotone, monosyllable
bi-	Two	bicycle, bilingual, bifunctional, bilateral
amphi-	both, on both sides, double, around	amphitheatre, amphibian (that lives in both water and on land)
pro-	forward, for	protect, project, pronoun

are relatively frequent, even in textbooks for lower grades. Similar tables can of course be made for important suffixes. Grade level, the students' needs, and the textbooks together provide direction for teachers in choosing words; preparing a word and morpheme pool provides considerable support.

The words to focus on are those students see in their textbooks. However, school texts contain too many new words for the teacher to teach (e.g., Hiebert et al., 2018) and therefore students need to develop their own strategies for deciphering words. One strategy is to get support from the context: if a student has no understanding of the word "broke", such a new word may be learned if the text say: "Peter was broke, he had no money to buy an ice cream" (so-called semantic bootstrapping). In other situations, morphological awareness may give the necessary support. If a student understands words like "breathless" and "homeless", the words "joyless" and "timeless" might be understood. Helping readers to attack new words effectively can be the key to their vocabulary and reading comprehension development.

How to work with students' morphological awareness

Preparing lessons to develop morphological awareness takes time. However, because vocabulary work can be planned across subjects, teachers can collaborate effectively and share knowledge. All teachers are responsible for supporting their students' vocabulary growth. Catherine Snow and her co-workers at Harvard University developed the programme "Word Generation", a programme used in several school districts in Boston where many students were at risk for developing reading disabilities as well as for school failure (e.g., Snow et al., 2009).[1] The "academic words" that students will meet repeatedly during their school years are chosen from the themes that are in focus each week during Grades 4 and 5. These themes and the words within them are introduced in 12 two-week units.

In grades 6–7 themes and words are introduced in 18 units, each unit lasting for one week and for 40–50 minutes each day. The different themes are introduced via video/TV. In addition, information from texts is to be discussed and read. The 5–10 "words of the week" are also presented on walls of the classrooms and throughout the school, to be used by students in both spoken and written language, Students are guided to understand both the structure and the meaning of these words in different contexts.

As mentioned previously I designed a programme of activities for developing morphological awareness in 5–6-year-old Norwegian children (Lyster, 2002). In order to deliver the intervention, teachers attended a morphological training course where they learned about the morphologic structure of Norwegian and of ways to support students. Discussions around the chosen words offered the teachers a tool for helping the students to develop morphological awareness. Some of the activities deal with compound words (e.g., understanding the meaning of words like "houseboat" and "boathouse") in which the main meaning changes when the parts change their place. In some compound words, a word will show up if the parts change their place, in others a nonsense word or a new word that might have a meaning is created (armchair> chairarm). To illustrate, what we did, for example, was use our two fists to mark the first word in "houseboat" (showing one fist while saying "house"). Then the other fist was added to the first one while we pronounced the last part, "boat", and then again the whole word "houseboat". Eventually the fists changed places while we told the children that the two parts changed places and asked them what word we then had. Activities with compound words can also easily be made on a flannel board, as shown in Figure 12.2, or in other ways by using a blackboard or flip-over. Figure 12.3 shows several tasks. When presenting such tasks to the children we usually worked with one task at the time so that easily distracted children could keep their attention to one picture or one word at a time.

Activities to promote morphological awareness are varied in the programme. Children learn, for example, to identify the prefix "un-" in "unhappy" by comparing "happy" and "unhappy". Words like this were also illustrated on the flannel board or blackboard. Also, we easily could add the comparative form and the superlative forms of adjectives and adverbs into our work. Figure 12.3 shows that the tiger is happi*er* than the figure next to him. He is the happi*est* of them all. Once understanding that the prefix *un-* gives a word like "happy" a meaning of "not happy", the children could figure out other words that could change meaning if *un-* was added to the beginning of the words.

They learned to listen to suffixes in the same way by identifying the phonological change when "hope" changed to "hopeless" and then figure out the

Learning words and understanding their morphological structures 119

Figure 12.2 Building compound words

Figure 12.3 Change meaning in the words

meaning of the new word. In the same way, children worked with grammatical morphemes such as plural *-s*, as shown in Figure 12.1, and verb endings: presentation of the word "walk" with the meaning of the word led to the introduction of the morphemes *-ing* and *-ed*, as in "walking" and "walked".

To illustrate with one more real case from my 2002 study: a 6-year-old boy was changing the two parts in "politibil" (police car). Before doing this operation the two parts in "police car" were identified by the teacher and small group of children who agreed that the last part carried the main meaning of the word. They also came up with other words made of two words that also ended with car ("minicar", "sidecar", "motorcar", and more). The boy, when he was asked to move the last part of "policecar" into the front of the word, came up correctly with "carpolice". He was asked if that was a word we used (*no* was the reply). However, when figuring out if the nonsense word "bilpoliti" (car police) could have some kind of a meaning, he was smiling broadly and said that "the word had to mean a police driving a car". Yes, this word that was not in the Norwegian vocabulary still had some meaning. What could we then say if the police were using a bike or motorbike? Children seem to love play-like activities with words, and the discussions about and playing with words like those described here was very popular.

Similar activities, both focusing on compound words, prefixes, and suffixes, can also be used successfully with older students and with children with special needs. Examples and a summary of activities are provided here.

Make a compound word: What word will you have if you put together "pea" and "soup"? (Each word can be illustrated by using the fists or two pieces of paper that first are shown apart when the single words are presented and then moved against each other for making the compound word.)
Ask what is left when one part of the word is deleted: What word is left if "pea" is deleted? (The corresponding fist or paper piece can be used to illustrate the part taken away.) The same activity can be done by deleting the part "soup" from "peasoup".
Ask what word they get when the two words in the compound word change their position: What word do we get if the words "pea" and "soup" change their places? (Use the fists or paper pieces as support to show how the words take other positions.)
Talk about the new word and if it is a real word: Is "soup-pea" a real word? What can it mean? Yes, it could be a special pea that is meant to be used in a soup. Sometimes, if the new word is not at all similar to a real word, it still can be explained by the last part, and the children can discuss the possible meaning of the nonsense word they have constructed.
Add or delete prefixes and suffixes: What word do you get if you ad *un-* to the front of "happy" (un-happy)? What is the meaning of this new word? What word do you get if you add *mis-* to the front of "understand" (*mis-*understand)? What is the meaning of the new word? What word do you get if you add *-less* to the end of "home" (home-less). What is the meaning of this new word? What word do you get if you add *-est* to the end of "strong" (strong-est)? What does this word mean? And so forth.
Discuss nouns' plural forms: Listen carefully, what is the difference between "car" and "cars" (say the two words slowly and rest a little on the sound /s/ when pronouncing "cars"). What difference does the /s/ make in the meaning of the word? Also, since the plural form in English can be

pronounced in different ways (allomorphs), as /s/ in "hats", /z/ in "dogs", and /iz/ in "keys", examples of all these pronunciations should be presented. It might be easier for young children to understand the meaning of the plural sounds if they can see the written root word/noun, see that the preschool or schoolteacher add the *s* at the end of the word and also be able to discover that this plural ending can be spoken in three different ways.

Discuss the tenses of verbs as well as the suffix *-s* and *-ing* in present form: Listen carefully, what happens to the word "walk" when I say, "Yesterday I walked to town". Also, as far as verbs are concerned, there are allomorphs; the same morpheme, with the same meaning and spelling, but with different pronunciations (jumped – wanted – fixed).

Present words with more than one morpheme that the children often meet. Talk about the word and its meaning and talk about the different morphological parts, their meanings, and what they add to the different roots.

When working with a certain prefix, find as many words as possible with the same appendix: *mis*take – *mis*behave – *mis*colour – *mis*trust – *mis*understand – *mis*use etc., *un*happy – *un*afraid – *un*acceptable – *un*armed – *un*believing – *un*clean – *un*friendly – *un*kind – *un*polished, and so forth. When working with suffixes, find as many words as possible with the same suffix: meaning*less* – shelter*less* – defence*less* – speech*less* – hope*less* – rest*less* etc., develop*ment* – engage*ment* – pay*ment* – amuse*ment* – govern*ment*, and so forth.

The way the words and affixes are chosen and their form depends on the mental age of the child and possible disabilities, as will the form of delivery of the teaching. Even if the child cannot read, they will be able to identify a plural *-s* in "cars" or the prefix *un-* in "unhappy" and see changes in a word's written form. The teacher may, for example, say, "Look, here I have written the word happy. Do you remember what happened to the word if we put *un-* in front of it? Yes, we got the word *un*happy. Here I have written the first part *un* so I also can add this part to the written word". However, some affixes are difficult to comprehend: for example, the prefix *con-*, meaning with/together. *Con-* is easily just seen as a syllable for the youngest children, since it is hard to figure out its meaning. There are many high frequency words, however, starting with this prefix: *con*cert, *con*text, *con*versation, *con*tribution, *con*cur, *con*tingent. Even if the meaning of *con-* is difficult to detect in some words, identifying such morphemes as orthographic structures (syllables) will also speed up word identification and give support to reading comprehension.

Vocabulary training may include finding words with the same meaning as a focus-word (synonyms) or words with the opposite meaning (antonyms). For example, "conflict" can be related to war, hostility, strife, etc., and words carrying the opposite meaning may be friendship, peace, harmony etc. A conflict may be solved through a conversation and cooperation. Putting the word in focus in a context and discussing its possible synonyms and antonyms will support children's vocabulary growth and the quality of their word knowledge.

122 Positive Special Education

Finally, visual support can be made to help students understand the meaning of different morphemes and how words are built by morphemes. Also, Melanie Walker elaborated further in her chapter (2024) about how such support can support students' language development as well as their reading and writing. Olivia Carter develop further in her chapter (2024) how working with language development in a group of students with special needs can be individualised at the same time as the classroom context is taken into account.

Summary

Systematic vocabulary teaching is effective for vocabulary development and children's spoken and written language development. Promising results from intervention studies show that morphological awareness training alongside vocabulary teaching is effective for typically developing children in mainstream and for those at risk for developing reading disabilities. Morphological awareness provides a solid basis for reading development, and morphological awareness can be an element in vocabulary interventions from an early age.

Acknowledgements

This chapter was originally published in Swedish in 2020. Some changes and additions have taken place, but most of the chapter is identical to the Swedish version. The contribution of Maggie Snowling to the English version of this chapter is acknowledged.

Note

1 The programme https://wordgen.serpmedia.org/elementary.html builds on what is known about how vocabulary develops.

References

Bourassa, D. C., & Treiman, R. (2008). Morphological constancy in spelling: A comparison of children with dyslexia and typically developing children. *Dyslexia*, 155–169.
Brinchmann, E. I., Hjetland, H. N., & Lyster, S. A. H. (2016). Lexical quality matters: Effects of word knowledge instruction on the language and literacy skills of third- and fourth-grade poor readers. *Reading Research Quarterly, 51*, 165–180.
Carter, O. (2024). Differentiated teaching. In M. Reichenberg, A.-K. Swärd & C. Shipton (Eds.), *Positive special education: Theory, applications and inspiration* (pp. 123–130). Routledge.
Hiebert, E. H., Goodwin, A. P., Cervetti, G. N. (2018). Core vocabulary: Its morphological content and presence in exemplar texts. *Reading Research Quarterly, 53*, 29–49.
Laws, G., Brown, H., & Main, E. (2016). Reading comprehension in children with down syndrome. *Reading and Writing, 29*, 21–45.
Lee, J., & Yoon, S. Y. (2017). The effects of repeated reading on reading fluency for students with reading disabilities: A meta-analysis. *Journal of Learning Disabilities, 50*, 213–224.

Lyster, S. A. H. (2002). The effects of a morphological versus a phonological awareness training in kindergarten on reading development. *Reading and Writing*, 15, 261–294.

Lyster, S. A. H., Lervåg, A. O., & Hulme, C. (2016). Preschool morphological training produces long-term improvements in reading comprehension. *Reading and Writing*, 29, 1269–1288.

Lyster, S. A. H., Snowling, M., Hulme, C., & Lervaag, A. (2021). Preschool phonological, morphological and semantic skills explain it all: Following reading development through a 9-year period. *Journal of Research in Reading*, 44, 175–188.

McGregor, K. K., Oleson, J., Bahnsen, A., Duff, D. (2013). Children with developmental language impairment have vocabulary deficits characterized by limited breadth and depth. *International Journal of Language & Communication Disorders*, 48, 307–319.

Næss, K. A. B., Melby-Lervåg, M., Hulme, C., & Lyster, S. A. H. (2012). Reading skills in children with down syndrome: A meta-analytic review. *Research in Developmental Disabilities*, 33, 737–747.

Reichenberg, M. (2024). Positive special education: Why are teachers' and students' self-efficacy important? Consequences for reading instruction and civic education. In M. Reichenberg, A.-K. Swärd & C. Shipton (Eds.), *Positive special education: Theory, applications and inspiration* (pp. 7–22). Routledge.

Snow, C. E., Lawrence, J. F., & White, C. (2009). Generating knowledge of academic language among urban middle school students. *Journal of Research on Educational Effectiveness*, 2, 325–344.

Walker. M. (2024). Using visuals and film to support literacy. In M. Reichenberg, A.-K. Swärd & C. Shipton (Eds.), *Positive special education: Theory, applications and inspiration* (pp. 88–94). Routledge.

13 Using a simple text to develop literacy in an inclusive classroom

Carolyn Harvey

In this chapter, I will show how using one visual text familiar to children can be used not only for enjoyment but also to draw out and develop several different literary based skills. The learning intention for this series of lessons is to be able write a story in the style of *Room on the Broom*, changing the context to be about a magic carpet ride. More able pupils should be encouraged to mimic the style of the original text using adventurous and descriptive language using the rhythm and rhyme of the text. Children with literacy difficulties will have opportunities to develop their vocabulary, reading skills, and writing in an inclusive lesson where they are part of a mixed ability group. The class should be split into groups and asked to write their own story for younger children in the school using the style of the text to create their own story about a magic carpet ride. The lesson plan allows all pupils to participate in the lesson regardless of their literacy ability.

The plan is broken down to include work at text, sentence and word level. This helps more able pupils develop and hone their grammatical skills and skills as young writers and furthermore allows pupils with literacy difficulties to work on development of early literacy skills. This lesson has been planned around the text *Room on the Broom* by Julia Donaldson although it is hoped that practitioners will be able to adapt the principles of this planning using other texts and stimuli.

The text

Room on the Broom tells the story of a friendly witch and her loyal cat who enjoy flying around on a broomstick. One day the wind blows the witch's hat off her head. Luckily a dog springs from the bushes with the hat in his mouth and asks to ride on the broom, and he joins her on the broom, and off they fly. It is not long before the witch loses the bow from her long ginger plait and her magic wand. Again, the witch is in luck, as a green bird and a clean frog retrieve them. To show how grateful she is, the witch makes room on her broom for them all. Then without warning the broom snaps in half, and the passengers tumble downwards into a bog, and a fiery dragon licks his lips at the thought of WITCH AND CHIPS! Bravely, the witch's new friends disguise themselves

Using a simple text to develop literacy 125

as a horrible beast to scare away the dragon and rescue the witch. The wonderful climax to the story sees A TRULY MAGNIFICENT BROOM rise from the witch's cauldron, cleverly designed with seats for everyone.

The text is really engaging for younger readers as it has a great rhythm and has elements of repetition which children can follow so they can join in with the reading. *Room on the Broom* is also full of rhyme, phonics, and punctuation! The illustrations are colourful, stylish, and support the understanding of the story.

Lesson 1

The objective for the week's lessons is to write a story in the style of *Room on the Broom* about a magic carpet ride. The class should be asked to write and illustrate the story for a younger class in the school.

Text level work

The aim of the first lesson is to familiarise the pupils with the story, giving plenty of opportunity for them to become acquainted with the style of writing.

The class would begin by reading the text.

Split the class into mixed ability groups. Each group should have a copy of the text and a large sheet of paper, marker pens, dictionaries, and a tablet or laptop connected to the internet.

The teacher should appoint a reader, scribe, illustrator, researchers, and reporters within each group. A set of tent cards with these roles written on would be a useful resource to have in the classroom for other lessons. The teacher should use his/her knowledge of the children's literacy abilities to assign appropriate roles.

Figure 13.1 Example tent card

The lesson content

The children should begin by reading the book or listening to the story being read on the laptop or tablet. On the second reading the scribe should note down the main events. The illustrators should record the story as a story board or sequence printed pictures from the story on a blank grid. Researchers should be looking for events to populate a blank writing frame (completed writing frame in the next section). Teachers could choose to provide sentences for pupils to sort if needed.

The scribes and illustrators would then match their work to the headings used on the writing frame.

As a rough guide:

Scribes – Higher ability
Readers – Average ability
Researchers – All abilities
Illustrators – Lower ability

At the end of the lesson the teacher should bring the class together to tell the story under each of the writing frame headings. Groups can either act out or tell their part of the story to the rest of the class. The teacher should tell the children that they will be planning their own story tomorrow about a magic carpet ride using the style of *Room on the Broom*.

Table 13.1 Writing frame

Opening   A witch is flying on a broomstick with her cat. The wind blows strongly, and she loses her hat.
First Event   A dog appears from the bushes with the hat in his mouth. He asks if he can ride on the broom with the witch, and they fly off over the fields.
Next event   A storm brews and the witch loses the bow from her long ginger plait. They fly down to the ground to look for it. There is suddenly a squawking noise and a green bird appears with the bow in his beak. The bird asks if there is room on the broom for him and off they go!
Next event   The storm continues, and the witch drops her wand. They land to look for the wand but can't find it. A frog appears from a pond with the wand and he joined the others on the broom and they flew over the mountains.
A crisis   The broomstick snaps in two, and everyone falls to the ground. There was a scary loud roar, and there was a mean dragon breathing fire saying that he wanted witch and chips for his tea.
Resolution   A big scary monster appears from the bog just as the witch is about to be eaten. The monster is in fact the dog, cat, frog, and bird covered in mud. The dragon was scared and flew off. The witch used her magic powers to create a new broom with seats for everyone!

Using a simple text to develop literacy 127

Lesson 2

Word level work

Children should continue to work in the same mixed ability groups. The aim of this lesson is for the pupils to explore the vocabulary that they may use when writing their magic carpet story. Again, the children will work at their own ability level all together in a group, with everyone's input contributing to the final story.

The teacher should begin by taking the class on a magic carpet ride. It may help to use the interactive white board or screen to show pictures, play music, and generally create an atmosphere. The children should then be sent to their groups with a large sheet of paper, which is going to be their magic word mat. On each table there should be prompt cards to help the children think of powerful vocabulary to write on the mat.

Readers should read one card at a time to the group, and scribes should write the words on the mat. Illustrators can contribute or draw on Post-it notes to add to the mat.

The illustrators should also have a chance to practise phonic skills by having a set of cards to read out that are at their stage of phonics acquisition – *hat, mat, gown, green, cloak. cried, roar, soar*, etc. – depending on individual ability.

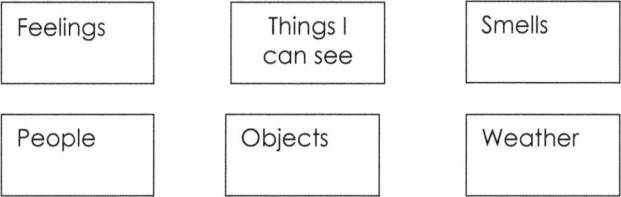

Figure 13.2 Example of prompt cards

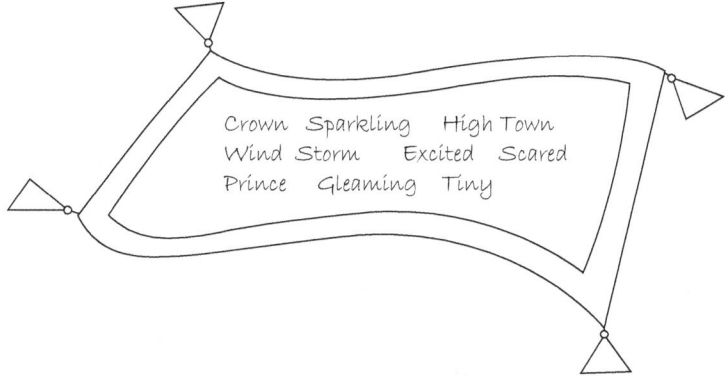

Figure 13.3 Practise phonic skills by cards to read

128 *Positive Special Education*

STORY BOARD

At the end of this lesson, pupils should have a chance to put some of their words into a sentence in preparation for writing their story.

Lesson 3

Text level work

Plan what will happen in your magic carpet story.

The groups will plan their story together using either the story board template or the writing frame.

Writing frame

First Event

Next event

Next event

A crisis
Resolution

The teacher should have some ideas cards which she can give to tables that are struggling to think what might happen in their own story.

By the end of the lesson, each group should have a plan for their magic carpet story.

Lesson 4

Sentence level work

The focus of the next lesson will be to write sentences in the style of *Room on the Broom*. Each group should be given a sentence from the original text as a prompt to construct their own sentences.

Here are some examples. I'm sure that the children will think of some brilliant ones too. During this activity the children who are working on their phonics skills should be encouraged to find rhyming words that can be used. Scribes and Readers should take charge of recording the sentences. Researchers should use the internet and dictionaries to help find words that rhyme and fit the style of the text.

The teacher will need to model a couple of sentences to the class and should then get the class as a whole to construct a sentence before the pupils go off to work in their groups.

The witch had a cat and a very tall hat
And long ginger hair that she wore in a plait

The prince had a crown and a long golden gown.
With long brown hair and a face with a frown.

Over the reeds and the rivers, they flew.
The bird shrieked with glee and the stormy wind blew.

Over the city the magic carpet flew.
His crown blew away as the carpet passed through.

Then all of a sudden from out of a pond
Leapt a dripping wet frog with a dripping wet wand.

All of a sudden from out of tower.
Sprang a beautiful princess holding a flower.

To end the lesson groups should swap their sentences with another group. Children should be asked to comment on one good feature of the sentence and one area for improvement.

Lesson five

This lesson should be a longer lesson where pupils have a chance to use their writing frames to write the magic carpet story for younger readers. Scribes and

Readers will be recording the ideas from the group, and Readers will be checking to see if the writing produced sounds like the original text. The Illustrators will draw pictures and write keywords to add to the story, while Researchers can use the internet to help find any words needed.

How is this lesson more inclusive than a traditional literacy lesson?

Children are working in mixed ability groups and can support each other's learning. Giving specific roles to every child helps them to be included in the work of the group. Pupils with particular strengths can be assigned a role that will allow them to use their strength, which should help to develop self-esteem. Children who find organisation difficult are supported through the series of scaffolded lessons. There is a clear framework for planning a story, support from a peer group, and chance to work on sentence and word level work before starting on the often daunting task of writing a story. The use of laptops and tablets appeals to many pupils, and furthermore poor readers and spellers gain confidence from being able to see and hear the spoken word rather than relying on being able to read or write.

The lesson provides opportunities for all pupils to work at their own level whether that is constructing and reading cvc words or using different narrative techniques to engage and entertain readers. There is enough scaffolding to support all learners and opportunities for more able learners to extend and develop their literacy skills.

14 Differentiated teaching

Olivia Carter

A teacher will be confronted with the task of differentiating the learning for a variety of needs and abilities throughout their career, whether working in SEND (Special Educational Needs and Disabilities) schools or in mainstream settings. This can seem daunting, initially. Teaching has moved on from "the one size fits all" approach, and inclusive teaching now emphasises a detailed focus on addressing the individual and targeting the specific learning needs of children. Each child is unique and learns in their own way, and it is therefore the task of us as teachers and educative practitioners to quickly and efficiently know our pupils and to acknowledge this need for differentiation. This will help to ensure the effective delivery of the curriculum and impact the best possible outcome for the students. In this chapter I will outline some examples from a literacy session which allows the reader to consider how it could be possible to effectively personalise the learning in one lesson and include a variety of pupils with SEND. The examples I bring aim to inspire the reader to reflect on their own classrooms as inclusive for all with a focus on using literacy that is visual.

The class context and lesson structure

While here at Swiss Cottage School we have designed our own curriculum to be more accessible and beneficial for our pupils, learning still needs to be adapted and personalised in each class. The lesson plan detailed next is targeted at a very diverse group of pupils in terms of their abilities. The class consists of those with mild learning disabilities who are developing early reading and writing skills, non-verbal pupils with autism and cognitive skills at the very earliest stages of development, and pupils with more profound physical disabilities who are limited to communicating with only their eyes, for example. This lesson was planned around the theme of belonging, with a specific focus on family.

Starter activity: 5 minutes

Although the class has varying needs and abilities, I plan for time for whole group integration sessions where possible to allow the learners the

DOI: 10.4324/9781003509141-14

opportunities to interact with each other and help develop social interaction and communication skills between peers. With this in mind, most lessons start as one whole group, and I introduce the topic in a way that appeals to all learners – often with a song or a medium that is visually appealing, such as an interactive game on the class whiteboard. This usually only lasts a few minutes, at most, as it is difficult to keep all ten learners actively engaged using the same approach. This starter activity generally lasts no more than five minutes, and I refer to strategies later that can be used to include all the children in this brief starter.

Main body of the lesson: children set off onto individual, paired, or smaller group tasks: 30–40 minutes

After the group introduction, the class will be split into three groups to work on their individual targets relating to the class theme. The theme for this particular lesson is "Belonging", and I have chosen the subtopic of "Family" as this is relevant to all learners. The week preceding the beginning of the new theme I contacted the learners' families to request photos to be sent in to use as resources for the lesson. This has the additional effect of providing an opportunity for families to be positively involved in their child's learning and enhances the meaning of the learning.

Group 1

Three learners with mild learning difficulties and one learner with more severe learning difficulties and cerebral palsy. The outcome of the lesson is for the learners with mild learning difficulties to be able to compose and type a variety of question words to be used in the following lesson in which they will role-play an interview that will be filmed.

Learning Intentions

(Learners A, B, and C)

1. *I can give the correct verbal response to a "who, what, or where" question using visual support.*
2. *I can work positively with a peer and contribute to a discussion.*
3. *I can open up a word document on the computer independently.*
4. *I can type three questions (who, what, and where questions) on a word document using the correct punctuation and space bar.*

(Learner D)

1. *I can navigate my way around my eye gaze and find the question words page.*
2. *I can work with a peer and contribute to the questions.*

Differentiated teaching 133

3. *I can respond to "who" and "where" questions using the eye gaze to give answers.*

Teacher/Practitioners – class teacher

The lesson will start with a brief recap of the question words they already know (what, who, and where) with the 4 MLD/SLD learners sitting at the horseshoe table in the centre of the classroom. I will use visuals as a prompt and start by asking each learner in turn, a question. The learner with CP uses an eye gaze device that enables him to access the same content and contribute independently to the activity. It is a speech generated device that allows him to use movement of his eyes to operate it. The eye gaze camera tracks the eye movement, which then moves the mouse on the screen, and the learner selects items either by holding their eye gaze for a certain time or by blinking.

Figure 14.2 shows how the page is displayed on the eye gaze. Each tab opens up a different page, and the child navigates with his eyes until he finds the correct page, and in this case Learner D understands that he needs to find the questions page in the literacy section and the family page in which he can respond to questions.

The four learners will split into two groups and work independently to compose and type three questions to ask their peers about their families. The outcome of this session is also for them to be able to work collaboratively with minimal adult support.

Figure 14.1 Eye gaze camera
Source: HelpKidzLearn.

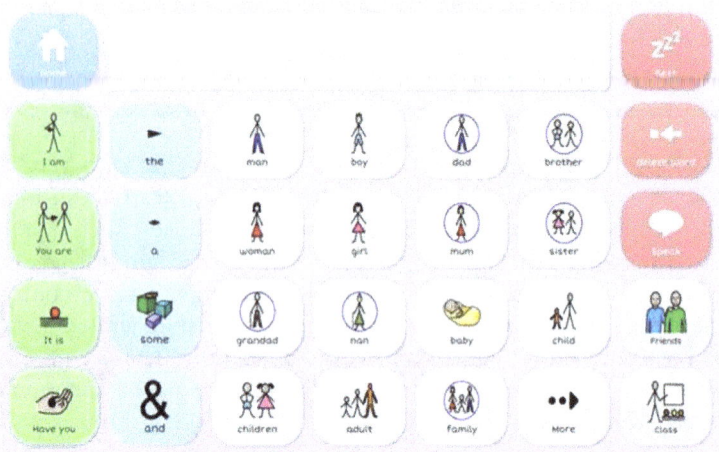

Figure 14.2 Each tab opens different pages
Source: HelpKidzLearn.

Group 2

Learner E – Non-verbal child with autism spectrum disorder (ASD)

Learning Intentions

1. *I can follow a simple verbal instruction.*
2. *I can construct a simple response to a question using a communication app on the iPad.*

Teacher/Practitioners – one teaching assistant

I have assigned a 1:1 adult for this learner as she needs the most support with listening and attention; the activity will be broken down into small chunks, and the learner will be given the opportunity to be rewarded frequently with the use of a behaviour board. The learner is highly motivated when using the iPad, so the tablet is used to its maximum effectiveness.

The adult will show Learner E a photo of her family member and verbally give a simple instruction such as "Put mummy in the box". Learner E will reposnd to the instruction with verbal prompting and place the photo of the family member in the box. The adult will then ask the question, "Where is Mummy/Daddy/Sister", and using the iPad with a commumuncation app installed on it, Learner E will construct a simple response – "Mummy in box". Similar to the eye gaze, the communicaiton app on the ipad is speech generated.

Figure 14.3 shows how the communication app is displayed on the iPad. The different colours represent pronouns, prepositions, and nouns, which helps the child to learn the important elements of a sentence and how to join them together in the correct order. As each tab is pressed, it activates a voice output, which gives the child immediate feedback.

Differentiated teaching 135

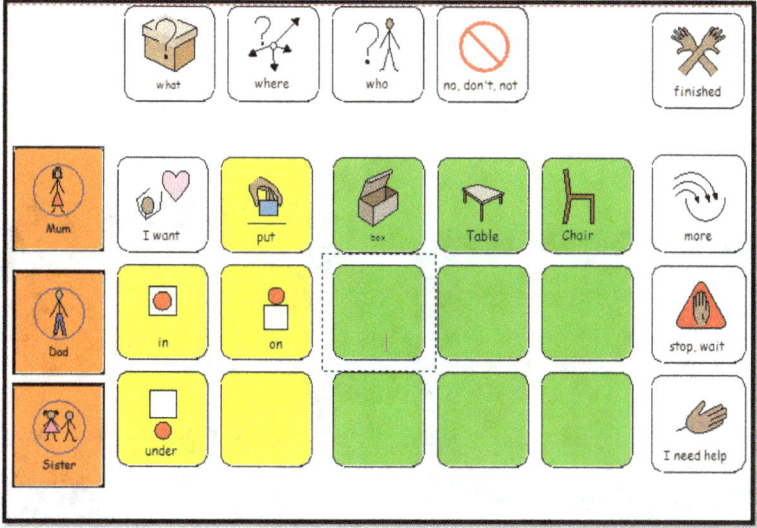

Figure 14.3 Communication app on the iPad
Source: HelpKidzLearn.

Group 3

Learner F and G – Global development delay and very low cognitive skills
Learner H – A child with cerebral palsy and low cognitive skills

Learning intentions

For this group I have broken down the learning objective to recognising pictures of their family. I am using a tool called "Choose It Maker" from a website called Helpkidzlearn.

Teacher/Practitioners – two teaching assistants

Helpkidzlearn is a collection of software for young children and those with learning difficulties to play online. You can edit and personalise learning materials to suit each child. It turns your text, images, and sounds into linear, on-screen choice, making activities that are accessible using a mouse, whiteboard, touch monitor, keyboard, or switches. The activities and games can then be downloaded onto an iPad. In this lesson, Learners F and G will be encouraged to use their hands to activate the tabs. For example, they will be asked to touch the photo of a family member from a choice of two tabs – one being just a colour and one being the photo. If they touch the correct tab, it immediately provides a reward of music and visuals.

136 *Positive Special Education*

Learner H, who has CP, doesn't possess the motor skills to be able to purposefully and independently activate a touch monitor with his hands. The most reliable movement he has is with his head. Therefore, a switch is attached to the headrest of his wheelchair to allow him to use movement of his head to make choices.

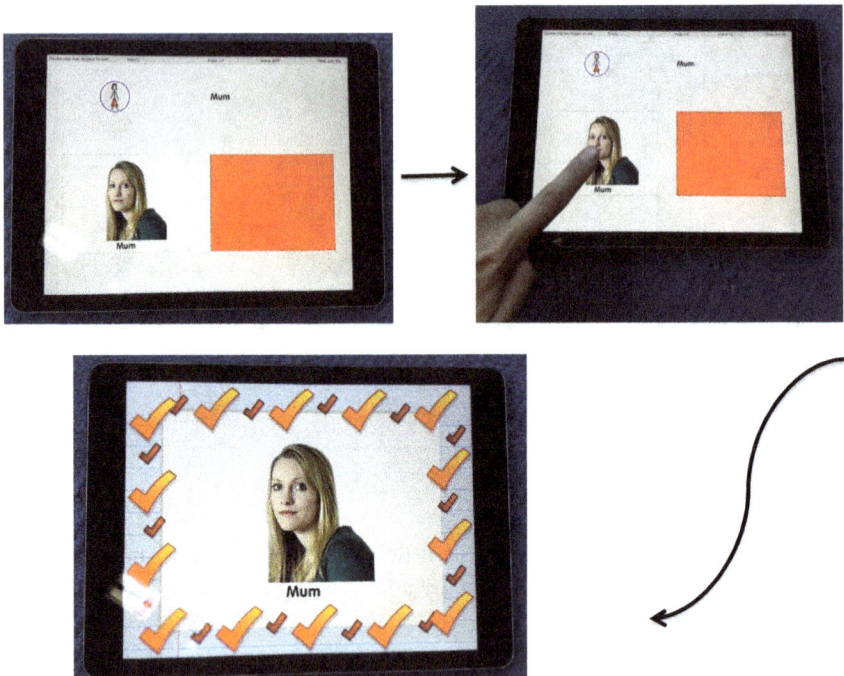

Figure 14.4 Game activity
Source: HelpKidzLearn.

Figure 14.5 Switch for the head
Source: HelpKidzLearn.

Differentiated teaching 137

Figure 14.6 Switch and the switchbox can operate the screen
Source: HelpKidzLearn.

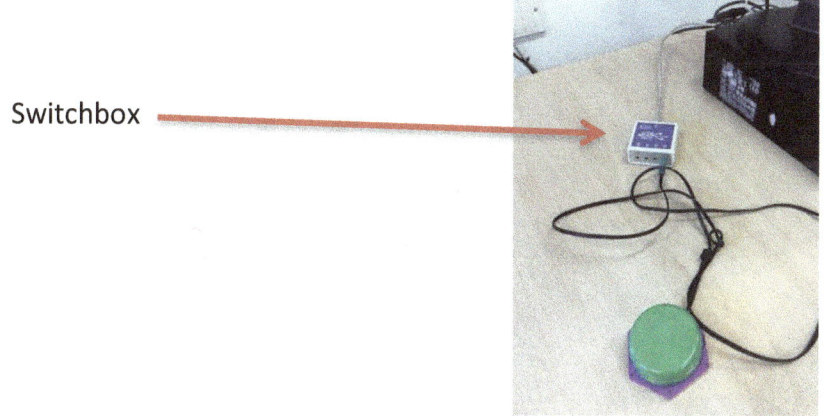

Figure 14.7 The switchbox

The switch is linked to a switchbox that connects to the computer that acts as a mouse. It automatically scans between the two tabs, and when the red frame is around the target tab, the learner is encouraged to press the switch in order to activate the reward.

Plenary

After the learners have completed their individual tasks (I usually allow 20–30 minutes for the main body of the lesson), I bring them all back as a group to celebrate the learning. During a lesson, we will often take photos and videos of the students engaging with their activities, and the content captured is used as a way to measure progress across the year. At the end of a lesson, I like to share the photos with the class to allow them to see their leaning and celebrate each other's achievements. This is something they all enjoy as they like recognising themselves and each other in the photos that are displayed on the class whiteboard. It is another opportunity for peer interaction and communication that provides further development in these fundamental skills.

15 The Witting method – safe, creative, and without textbook

Louise Wramner and Ann-Katrin Åkerman

In the 1960s when Maja Witting was new in her profession as a teacher, she was asked to teach reading and writing to a student in sixth grade whose earlier efforts had been in vain. Her more experienced colleagues could not recommend any untried method because to their knowledge everything had been tried. And so it came about that Maja Witting instead chose to rely on the student and his reactions when trying to find a way to work. She made an agreement with the student that he was to give her all the information he could. They decided to step by step try different elements in the work he had earlier been subject to, and the student agreed to give his teacher truthful reactions to the different things they tried. Realising that the student was her best source of information, Maja Witting kept a close record of his reactions, and little by little they together formed a working routine, eliminating every non-useful element, saving the parts that proved useful. The student preferred to work with "nonsense words", and his recurrent comment was as follows: "With them I can do one thing at a time. Instead of both reading the symbols and trying to think of the word at the same time".

But since written language is basically communication, Maja Witting found it impossible to separate content and technique, but in the long run she could do nothing but accept the fact that the material to work with had to consist of what later came to be called "content neutral language structures".

Once the idea had proven itself useful in practice, it wasn't difficult to find support for it when analysing the reading and writing processes. Developing the method was a process of about ten years during which the ideas were used together with several new students. Other teachers tried to work in the same way, and students and teachers were pleased with the results. Maja Witting now had a method based both on multiple experiences and on a theory of reading and writing. Central in her method is the firm belief that every student can learn to read and write. With the help of the method, it is possible to support the students' use of their intrinsic will to learn and their belief in their own ability. This means that the Witting Method can be seen as an example of positive special education.

Among Maja Witting's many books, *Vägledning i det praktiska metodarbetet* (Witting, 2000), which is the teacher's handbook, and *Wittingmetodens idébakgrund* (Witting, 2005), which presents the theoretical background, are the most important. Maja Witting later became employed at the teacher training college at Uppsala University, responsible for learning to read and write.

A Swedish dissertation concerning the method has been presented by Swärd (2008).

The actual classroom work

If you visit a Swedish classroom where the teacher has chosen to work in accordance with Maja Witting's Method, you will not find any textbooks for learning to read, but you will always find and recognise two central activities.

The first, *Attentive Writing*, being short and strict, is a repeated routine the students follow together: the object being to create an automatic connection between the language sounds and their symbols.

The second, *Creative Word Search*, is never the same, being based on the students' active participation using each one's own individual spoken language capacity, and the object is to broaden the linguistic competence of the students.

Our next examples derive from our own pedagogical wisdom and teaching experiences in the classroom.

Attentive writing

The students are ready with pen and paper. They all face the teacher, focusing on and waiting for what they are going to hear from the teacher.

The teacher, just as focused as the students, says for example: [mi:]. The students repeat the sounds out loud. And then turning inwards, they each listen to the soft echo of the sounds they can perceive inside their heads. They turn to the paper and write the symbols they know represent the given sounds. They look at what they have written, at the same time hearing it echo again inside themselves. They then look up and wait for the next combination of sounds to be pronounced by the teacher.

The routine continues with maybe ten new combinations for example [pi:], [du:], [nɑ:].

Student comments about the work

The *Attentive Writing* might sound monotonous and uninteresting, but according to students it is not.

> *I can feel the sounds in my brain.*
> *I get rid of other thoughts. I can concentrate. I just listen to the sounds.*
> *In the beginning I just "saw" the letters. I can hear now.*
> *I can find the sounds in my mouth.*
> *It makes my pronunciation better.*
> *I feel safe because the exercise is always done the same way.*
> *My brain goes: Aha!*

The students seem to appreciate the way the routine helps them to concentrate and feel confident. They like the slow pace, giving them time to feel, hear, and pronounce the sounds and to write the symbols. To be able to feel the brain work is a new and important experience. These are all reasons for the built-in steps in the routine the method uses to facilitate the *automation* of the sound-symbol connection.

Creative word search

After the Attentive Writing they move on to the second central activity: the Creative Word Search. It is time to focus on exploring and developing the students' oral language competence, further described and developed in the chapter by Ann-Katrin Swärd (2024).

Starting from a single sound or a combination of sounds like the ones the students just met in the Attentive Writing routine, the object now is for each one to find words starting with the given sounds. Sometimes the students find many words, sometimes maybe only one or two. Regardless of which, their words will do.

(In the text later, Swedish words are written in bold letters and the English translation within parentheses. The teacher's lines are written in italics.)

- *Do you have a word starting with the sounds [pi:]?*
- **Pia**
- *What do you think of when you say **Pia**?*
- I think of my sister, and her name is **Pia.**
- **Pipa** (Eng: pipe).
- *What do you think of when you say **pipa**?*
- My grandfather smokes a **pipa.**
- **Pil** (Eng: arrow/street arrow/dart/willow)
- *What do you think of when you say **pil**?*
- I can throw **pilar** (Eng: darts) at a **piltavla** (Eng: dartboard).
- *Can that word mean anything else?*
- I don't think so.
- It can also be a tree: **pil** (Eng: a willow).
- And you have to follow a **pil** (Eng: street arrow) so you know where to go.
- **Pilbåge** (Eng: bow)
- *What are you thinking of when you say **pilbåge**?*
- I use a **pilbåge** together with **pilar** (Eng: arrows).
- **Pina** (Eng: pain, torment, anguish – verb and noun).
- *What do you think of when you say **pina**?*
- I don't know, but I have heard the word.

  (None of the other students knows the meaning of **pina** so they are asked to go home and ask if anybody can explain the word.)

- **Pilot** (Eng: pilot).
- *What do you think of when you say **pilot**?*

- I want to be a **pilot** and fly a plane.
- **Piano** (Eng: piano)
- *What do you think of when you say **piano**?*
- I can play the **piano.**
- **Pirat** (Eng: pirate) is also a word beginning with [pi:].
- *What are you thinking of then?*
- **Pirater** (Eng: pirates) hijack ships.
- *Let us now try to create a story from the words you have found. I'll be your secretary. What do you want your story to be about?*
- About Pia and her grandfather.
- *What does Pia do?*
- She plays the piano while waiting for her grandfather.
- Her grandfather is a pilot.
- *What does the grandfather do?*
- He follows the street arrows to find his way to Pia.
- *Why does he want to visit her?*
- Because it's her birthday.
- *Does he bring a gift?*
- He brings a bow and arrows.
- *What happens then?*
- Pia and her grandfather shoot arrows with the bow in the garden where a willow grows.
- *Who is winning?*
- Pia wins.
- *And what does her grandfather do?*
- He smokes a pipe and reads Pia a story about pirates.

A discussion between the students and the teacher results in the following story.

Pia and her grandfather

Pia plays piano while waiting for her grandfather.
He is a pilot.
He follows the street arrows to find his way to Pia.
It is Pia's birthday.
She gets a bow and arrows from her grandfather.
They shoot arrows with the bow in the garden where a willow grows.
Pia is winning.
Then grandfather smokes a pipe and reads Pia a story about pirates.

The next day a student beaming with joy reveals having found a new word: **pir.** (Eng: pier), and another student brings an explanation of the word **pina** (Eng: pain, anguish, torment). "It's when something hurts you or is really, really boring".

Student comments about the work

In our experience students like this creative part of the classroom work.

> *I didn't know I had all those words!*
> *It makes me start to really think.*
> *It's fun to look for words and then make up stories with those words.*
> *You learn new words and at the same time learn to pronounce them well.*
> *You learn to write sentences with the correct word order with the help of the teacher and the other students in the class.*
> *You can use your brain, think extra, you refresh your brain.*

The students notice, once again, how the work activates their brains and that they also learn new words from each other. They experience that a word can have several different meanings and that we all know words we don't know the meaning of. A passive word becomes an active part of your vocabulary. Sometimes a word can be misinterpreted or not correctly pronounced. The Creative Word Search offers opportunities to explain and correct.

The students also notice how word order can sometimes play a crucial role when creating sentences.

With the help of questions from the teacher, a story line and a suitable heading can be created which will serve as models for future text writing.

The teacher saves sentences, and texts for the students to enjoy reading later once they can read on their own. Common beginner books with texts and pictures assume that everyone thinks the same way and interprets pictures in the intended way. The pictures are often meant to support the students in the decoding of the words. This means, for instance, that a picture of a bicycle wheel might cause the student to read "tire", "spokes", or "hub" instead of the intended word "wheel". This is one of the Witting method's arguments for not using textbooks or premade illustrations, also further elaborated in the chapter by Ann-Katrin Swärd (2024) and Wramner (2020).

The reading and writing processes

The two parts of the classroom work *Attentive Writing* and *Creative Word Search* are based on Maja Witting's experiences from working with students. To theoretically justify using writing instead of reading in the initial stages, she felt the need for a careful analysis of both reading and writing processes.

She formulated her analysis as follows:

Reading
R (Reading) = S (Symbol function) × C (Comprehension)

Writing
W (Writing) = CC (Content Creation) × S (Symbol function)

144 *Positive Special Education*

A corresponding analysis and a similar formula on reading was later (1986) presented by Gough and Tunmer, known as The Simple View of Reading:

R (Reading with comprehension) = D (Decoding ability) × C (listening Comprehension)

When learning to read and write it is preferable if the two parts – sound-symbol function and the ability to comprehend, or to create content – can be developed according to their different characters.

The symbol function requires accuracy but is not complicated, and what you must learn is rather limited. You need an automatic connection between a certain number of sounds and their symbols, the reading direction from left to right and consonance. An automatic technique, serving both reading and writing, can be achieved using the *Attentive Writing*.

The comprehension/content creation has a different character: it is creative and personal. You can enjoy the content of any text that refers to things you know and uses words you are familiar with, and you can talk about the things you have experienced with your own words.

The *Creative Word Search* makes it possible for the students to work orally to develop their language without being limited by not yet mastering the symbol function.

You cannot successfully work textbook in the initial stages. Mixing symbol function and comprehension/content creation will make learning difficult for students where it should (and could) be easy and also restrict students where they should be able to feel their individual freedom.

With *the Content Neutral Language Structures* all students can work with their language competence on its terms and with the symbol function on its terms and still experience the close connection between the two, which together constitute reading and writing.

The content neutral language structures

The heart of this method, and its unique feature, is the use of the Content Neutral Language Structures, which make it possible to learn to read and write by *writing* instead of by *reading*.

The structures are combinations of vowels and consonants conforming to the Swedish language. All symbols are always used in their basic sound-symbol relationship. Deviations from the basic alphabetical one to one relationship is excluded. A /k/ is always [k] and an /i/ is always [i:]. In Swedish this gives us combinations such as the following: si, pa, se, ym, of, krys sme, dru, klam, svip, lepa, buti. They are all *structures that appear normally in the Swedish language*.

The order in which the sound-symbol connections are included in the material is the following: vowels – a, i, o, e, ö, å, y, ä, u; consonants – l, s, m, p, f, k, v, t, r, b, n, g, j, d, h. Similar symbols or sounds are kept as far apart as possible. Symbols without a sound of their own (c, q, w, x, and z) are introduced later. All kinds of inconsistent spelling are introduced when the basic symbol function is in place.

In every similar language, such as English, there is a kernel of phonetical spelling possible to use as material for Content Neutral Language Structures that can be used in Attentive Writing and Creative Word Search when working with reading and writing instruction.

There are several advantages when using these structures instead of texts. (1) They give you an unlimited amount of practice material and unwanted guessing – instead of decoding – can be avoided. (2) The pace in acquiring the technique can be adjusted to the students' needs without limiting their oral language development. (3) You can work on two different levels at the same time. (4) Technique of coding and decoding can stay on a very simple level, while content can be worked on at a higher level corresponding to the student's own oral language competence. (5) The work also improves the students' pronunciation.

All of this means that it is possible to use the Witting method with different types of students: young first-time learners, slow learners, students with intellectual disabilities or with a different first language, as well as dyslexic students at any level, at school or university.

Preparatory work

Before the students can even start to work with the symbols, we need to make sure they are well prepared. The preparations involve different abilities.

Independence work and student learning responsibility

It is important that the students are responsible for their own learning. When young students start school, the teacher discusses with each of them what activities they can do on their own without assistance.

The students ask themselves, "What can I do on my own without asking for help?" The answer might be, "I can draw, cut, sew, do jigsaw puzzles, listen to books", and so on. Their suggestions are then used as *Independence Work*. They are not only working on their own, more important is that they develop their feeling of self-confidence and independence.

A student who knows what it feels like to be comfortable when working can also inform the teacher if something is unclear or if any uncertainties arise in any part of the schoolwork. In this way, a problem can be dealt with before it becomes a major problem. The students' information must of course be met with interest on the part of the teacher.

The slow progress and the small steps are also important ingredients in helping the students follow their own learning. The students develop a metacognitive ability, and they can take on their learning responsibility. The student's independence work also provides meaningful activity for the student while awaiting the teacher's attention further elaborated in the chapter by Ann-Katrin Swärd (2024).

Words need to be based on experience

Reading comprehension is closely connected to, and dependent on, the depth of the students' own spoken language vocabulary. Therefore, it is essential to help them develop real concepts of as many words as possible. For example, to form a real concept of the word "alley", you need to visit an alley. When you are walking in an alley, you can almost touch the houses on either side with your hands, and you can listen to how it sounds when you shout in the alley. In the same way, the difference between, seeing a picture of a flower, and touching, smelling, handling an actual flower, is immense. It is also important to help the students carefully describe the things they see, smell, touch, and handle, and the depth of the students' future reading comprehension depends on this.

Written language differs from oral language

There are differences between oral and written language. Therefore, it is important that students have the possibility to listen to written language. Reading to children is always recommended to parents and to preschool teachers, an activity will be further developed in the chapter by Ann-Katrin Swärd (2024) and Halaas Lyster (2020) also see as essential. It is just as important to let the students listen to good books for their enjoyment at school.

The language sounds

The students need to get to know the language sounds. To start, they focus on, listen to, identify, and name sounds in the classroom, in the garden, street, and so on. The students can also be asked to produce sounds themselves – such as rattling keys, cutting paper, bouncing a ball – and then discuss how each different sound can be described and named.

The next step is learning to hear the individual language sounds in their own language. This work is only oral. The teacher asks, for instance:

- What sounds the same in the words få, så, må, rå, tå?
- Can you hear an [i:] in the following words: liv, mig, sur, glad, ris? (one word at a time)
- Can you find words where you hear: [m], [l], [k]? (one sound at a time)

Turning language sounds into symbols

After this preparatory work, it is time to start focusing on the symbol function. First of all, each individual language sound is to become connected to its symbol.

The students listen to a short story containing many words with one particular sound; and the story concludes with a word ending with the sound in question. After having focused on and pronounced this last sound, the students listen to the story again, disregarding its content, focusing on hearing that particular sound in the words of the story.

Then it is time to learn to write the symbols in a way that excludes the possibility of misinterpreting one letter for another.

Back to the students' own oral language, they are now asked to try finding words with the language sound they have just focused on. If the sound is [s], the students might find *sko* (Eng: shoe), *små* (Eng: small), *stora* (Eng: big), *svarta* (Eng: black), *smutsiga* (Eng: dirty), *skokräm* (Eng: shoe polish). These words can be used to create a short story to illustrate. The alliteration will usually please the students.

Skor kan vara små, stora och svarta.	Shoes can be small, big, and black.
Skor kan vara smutsiga.	Shoes can be dirty.
Då måste man putsa dem med skokräm.	Then you must polish them with shoe polish.

The symbol function also includes direction from left to right and consonance. The consonance exercise is carried out in the following way: The teacher writes an /a/ and an /l/ approximately 50 cm apart on the board and asks the students to pronounce the two sounds. The teacher then points to the /a/, and the students are asked to hold the a-sound while the teacher slowly moves the finger to the /l/, and they switch over to the l-sound. The exercise is repeated several times, but each time the distance between the /a/ and the /l/ is reduced. Finally, /a/ and /l/ are next to each other and the students manage to "read" from left to right with consonance without difficulty.

The sound-symbol connections, the reading direction, and consonance must be practised repeatedly to become automated. This ensures that in future reading and writing all energy can be spent on comprehension and content creation.

Additional goals

The basic aims of this method are to help the students *learn to read and write* and to *develop their language*, but the work leads to more than that.

Linguistic awareness

When it comes to developing the students' linguistic awareness the different parts in the method play their obvious parts. (a) *Phonological awareness* is already established in the preparatory work and continues into both the Attentive Writing and the Creative Word Search. (b) *Morphological and semantic awareness* increase with the help of the word discussions and the building of sentences and texts. The importance of morphological awareness is also stressed by Halaas Lyster (2020). (c) Both *syntactic* and *pragmatic awareness* are developed by the Creative Word Search.

The use of multiple senses

Whatever you want to learn, it needs to somehow become part of yourself. This method strives to help the students to engage all senses possible. In the Attentive Writing hearing is of course essential, and you can feel your mouth produce the sounds and your hand create the symbols. It also gives the students time to shape the symbols to their satisfaction – and provide a pleasing and clear result to their vision.

The hearing-impaired students can also benefit from the Attentive Writing. By studying and copying how the teacher produces the different language sounds, they, too, can manage to produce the sounds even if they cannot hear them and link them to their symbols.

Know and trust your own ability

The students' own ability to use spoken language is used as the working material, and the exploration of the language is based on their own words. This gives them the feeling that what they already know is valuable – providing a safe foundation for the student's true feeling of competence and giving them access to their inherent will to investigate and explore.

Being part of a group, working with the Attentive Writing or the Creative Word Search, lets the students experience the different ways we can all learn – individually, from each other, and together. Such experiences strengthen one's inherent drive to be part of a collaborative process.

All in all, the Witting method strengthens the students' will to learn and their feeling of being capable of success. And mastering things for their own sake becomes rewarding in itself which will be further elaborated in the chapter by Monica Reichenberg (2024).

Teacher comments on working with the Witting method

This text has hopefully given you a picture of the Witting method: its theory, the preparatory work, the Content Neutral Language Structures, the Attentive Writing, and the Creative Word Search. We leave you with two quotes from teachers reflecting on why they chose to work with the Witting method.

> When I started studying the Witting Method, I suddenly realized why some of my students didn't learn, and I found tools to prevent it from happening again. I also got tools to help the students who had failed before they entered junior high.
>
> With the Witting Method, I can involve the whole class, the "whole" student and the entire school subject of Swedish. No one is left in the lurch, and no one gets bored. It is creative and exciting, but we don't ignore details and accuracy.

References

Gough, P. B., & Tunmer, W. E. (1986). Decoding, reading and reading disability. *Remedial and Special Education, 7*, 6–10. SAGE.

Halaas Lyster, S.-A. (2020). Att lära om ord och ordens morfologiska struktur. In A. -K. Swärd, M. Reichenberg & S. Fischbein (Eds.), *Positiv specialpedagogik Teorier och tillämpningar*. Studentlitteratur.

Reichenberg, M. (2024). Positive special education: Why are teachers' and students' self-efficacy important? Consequences for reading instruction and civic education. In M. Reichenberg, A.-K. Swärd & C. Shipton (Eds.), *Positive special education: Theories, applications and inspiration* (pp. 7–22). Routledge.

Swärd, A.-K. (2008). *Att säkerställa skriftspråklighet genom medveten arrangering. Wittingmetodens tillämpning i några olika lärandemiljöer*. Specialpedagogiska institutionen, Stockholms universitet. http://www.avhandlingar.se/om/Ann-Katrin+Sw%C3%A4rd/

Swärd, A.-K. (2024). Positive special education: Challenge students to read and write in a creative way without fixed material. In M. Reichenberg, A.-K. Swärd & C. Shipton (Eds.), *Positive special education: Theories, applications and inspiration* (pp. 95–103). Routledge.

Witting, M. (2000). *Vägledning i det praktiska metodarbetet*. Förlaget Verti AB.

Witting, M. (2005). *Wittingmetodens idébakgrund*. Ekelunds förlag.

Wramner, L. (2020). Blodanalysen var normal – det kunde jag läsa alldeles själv. In A.-K. Swärd, M. Reichenberg & S. Fischbein (Eds.), *Positiv specialpedagogik Teorier och tillämpningar*. Studentlitteratur.

Index

ability: considerations for teacher 27–30; feedback and 26–27; implicit theories about 23–30; influenceable 25–27; know and trust your own 148; notions of ability as fixed or changing 24–25; skills and 23
academic words 115, 116, 118
adaptive teaching 64–72
Agran, M. 16–17
Åkerman, A.-K. 59
"All About Me and My Community" 64
alternative communication 47, 106
analogue programming 60, 61
Andersson, M. 55, 56
Antonovsky, Aaron, sense of coherence and 4, 54, 108
Archdale School 44–52; capabilities developed through narrative at 44–52; conclusion 51–52; environment for learning at 49; first languages spoken by students at 44; inclusion at 45–51; learning intentions and 46–48; parental involvement at 45; participation and engagement at 48–49; student ethnicities present at 45; teaching expressive communication to pupils with SEND at 63–72
arithmetic *see* mathematics
ASCII table 59
assessment: of abilities 10, 11, 14, 25–26, 28–30; of decoding images 87; digital tools for 54; of independence in transportation 83; for learning opportunities, questions for 87; plan, in using visuals and film to support literacy 97–98; programming for 60; questioning as assessment prompts 100; SCEETS 50; teacher's role in 108; through role play 100
Attention Autism 48–49, 65, 71, 72
Attentive Writing 140–141, 143, 144, 145, 147–148
attitudes 3, 9–11, 13, 17, 24, 29, 35, 37
attribution theory *see* positive psychology
augmented communication 47
autism spectrum disorder (ASD) 4, 13, 46, 131, 134; Attention Autism 48–49, 65, 71, 72
avatars 56

Bandura, Albert 2; clarification to the concept of self-efficacy by 11–12; conceptualisation of self-efficacy beliefs 12; on importance of self-efficacy 7–8; optimistic beliefs and 4, 8, 11, 16; sources influencing extent of individual's self-efficacy 13–14
Beach, Dennis 26, 29
Boaler, J. 28
bound morphemes 112–113
Brinchmann, E. I. 115
British teachers 7, 18, 19
bug 59, 60, 61

capability approach 1, 3, 10, 18
Carr P. B. 23, 24, 27
Carter, Olivia 38, 122
"Choose It Maker" 135
civic education: reading instruction and, consequences for 7–20; teachers' self-efficacy influencing teaching and outcomes of 16–17, 19
cognitive skills 131, 135
cognitive strategies 38
coherence 4, 54, 108
collaborative learning 38

collective learning 105
collective self-efficacy 12
communication skills: differentiated teaching and 132; expressive 63–64, 69, 72; visuals and film to support 96, 101
community activities: applications of functional literacy 74–82; independence of pupil and 83; independent transportation 17–19, 74–84; to support participation 19
compound words 113–114, 116, 118, 119, 120
comprehension 96, 100, 144
Compulsory School for Pupils with Intellectual Disabilities 61
confidence 4, 7, 9, 12–13, 18–20, 27, 36, 57, 72, 74, 83, 84, 86, 87, 90, 93, 96, 107, 108, 109, 112, 130, 141, 145; *see also* self-confidence; self-efficacy
content creation 144
content-neutral language structures 105, 110, 139, 144–145, 148
cooperative learning 38, 39
core learning 46–47, 49, 51
Creative Word Search 140, 141–143, 144, 145, 147, 148
curriculum: ability and, implicit theories about 30; actively engaging in 48–49; environment for 49–51; learning intentions 46–48; national 32–33, 42; programming 59; semi-formal and informal 46, 48, 49, 50, 63, 65; teaching expressive communication to pupils with SEND 63–64
curriculum pathway 46–50, 63

Davies, Gina 48, 72
decoding 8, 87, 143, 144, 145
Delta model 34
democracy 16–17, 105
Department for Education 64
derivational morphemes 113
descriptive writing 93–94
devaluation 10, 11
Dewey, John 16; *see also* civic education
differentiated teaching 131–138; *see also* Swiss Cottage School Model
difficulties 4, 8, 14, 15, 16, 19, 24, 56–58, 63, 65, 86, 100, 103, 106, 107, 109, 112, 124, 132
digital competence 59

digital narratives 55–59; interactive quiz 57; interactive stories 56–57; quiz walks with QR codes 58; verbal presentation through an avatar 56; virtual reality (VR) 58–59
digital tools 54–61; avatars 56; digital narratives 55–59; interactive quiz 57; interactive stories 56–57; as a pedagogical tool 54–55; programming 59–61; quiz walks with QR codes 58; virtual reality (VR) 58–59
discrediting 10, 11
Donaldson, Julia 124
Down syndrome 63, 112
Doyle, Sir Arthur Conan 96
Dweck, Carol: fixed mindset and 5, 24; growth mindsets AND 4–5, 15, 55; implicit theories of ability AND 23–30

Early Career Framework 64
Early Learning and Educational Technology Policy Brief 55
Early Years Foundation Stage 63
ECCOM (Early Childhood Classroom Observation Measure) 108–109
Education and Health Care Plan (EHCP) 46, 47, 49, 50, 86
Education Endowment Foundation 64
emotional regulation 46, 50, 72
emotional states 14
entity theories of intelligence 24
Equals Curriculum 63
Erstad, O. 58
ethnic minority groups 10, 45
evidence-based arguments 88
expectations 9, 10, 11, 14, 18, 27, 35, 64, 65, 72
expressive communication, teaching to pupils with SEND 63–72

feedback 26–27
Fitzgerald, J. 106
fixed mindset 5, 24
Florin, K. 109
free morphemes 112–113
functional literacy: applications of, in the community 74–82; digital narratives and 58; independence in transportation and 17–19, 74–84; practical activity for all pupils 83; teachers' self-efficacy influencing

152 *Index*

teaching in 17–19; teaching, to pupils with SEN 74–84
functional reading *see* functional literacy

global success factors 2, 3
Google Maps 75–80
Gough, P. B. 144
grammatical morphemes 113, 114, 119
grammatical skills 124
growth mindsets: digital tools for developing 55; from optimistic beliefs to 4–5; teacher self-efficacy to promote 15
Guardian, The 20n2
Gudiño, R. 86; *see also* inclusive literacy
Guo, Y. 15

Helpkidzlearn 135
Henderlong Corpus, J. 26
Hiebert 113
Hjertø, K. B. 34
Hjetland, H. N. 115
Hound of the Baskervilles, The (Doyle) 96–102
Hugo, M. 108

Ibrahimović, Zlatan 2
ICD-11 46
ICT (Information and Communication Technology): in adaptive teaching 64, 72; for independent travel 75, 83; skills 75
implicit theories of ability 23–30; considerations for teacher 27–30; feedback and 26–27; influenceable 25–27; notions of ability as fixed or changing 24–25; skills and 23
IMTEC 34
inclusive education 17, 49; change in teaching methods 37–38; educational practices and challenges 36–37; inclusion, defined 45–46; inclusive optimistic approach to 32–43; leadership situation and challenges 34–38; learning intentions and 46–48; organisational situation and challenges 35; self-efficacy and 17; station method 38, *39*, 39–40; typical school day 39–42
inclusive literacy 85–95; comments 92–95; descriptive writing 93–94; ideas for further activities 93; keywords and symbols 90; lesson activities and links to learning intentions 88–89; lesson content and structure, overview of 86–92; questions, questioning, and attention to detail 87–88; sentence builder 92; specific activities 89–92; telling the story with visual support 91; who is doing what 92
inclusive teaching 38; civic engagement and 17; consequences for 7–20; reading instruction and 7, 16, 103; teachers' self-efficacy influencing teaching and outcomes of 16–17, 19
incremental theories of intelligence 25
independence: adaptive teaching and 70, 72; communicative, for employment and life skills 96; of pupil in the community 83; quiz walks with QR codes and 58; teacher development and 37; in transportation 17–19, 74–84; verbal presentations and 56; work and student learning responsibility 145
independent skills 72, 98
Informal Curriculum 63
intellectual disability (ID): ability to travel for people with 17–19; barriers to voting for people with 17; digital tools for 54; learned optimism and 2; learning words and understanding morphological structures 112; models and 7–10; reading and writing without fixed material 105, 109; subcategories of, in ICD-11 46
intelligence, theories of: entity 24; incremental 25
interactive quiz 57
interactive stories 56–57
internal success factors 2, 3
intervention study 3, 17, 105

Johansson, Anna 5, 15
Johansson, I. 107, 110
Jonsson, Anna-Carin 5, 15, 109
Jordan, Michael 2

Kappel, Alexandra 5, 15
Karlstad model 110n1

labelling 10
language skills *see* literacy
language sounds 146; turning into symbols 146–147; in Witting method 105, 140, 146–147, 148

language structures, content-neutral 105, 110, 139, 144–145, 148
learned helplessness 2, 4
learned optimism 2, 3
learning capacities 8–11; *see also* capability approach; medical model; social model
Lepper, M. R. 26
life skills 3, 96
linguistic awareness 103–104, 107, 147
linguistic development 103, 107
listening skills *see* speaking and listening skills
literacy: functional literacy, pupils with SEN and 74, 81, 83; inclusive 85–95; text to support 124, 130; visuals and film to support 96–102; *see also* reading skills; writing skills
Litwen, E. 49
Louvet, S. 60
Lyster, Halaas 146, 147

Maguire, Matt 5, 18, 106
Mandela, Nelson Rolihlahla 7
map skills 60
Marcone, V. 86
Mar Galcerán 20n2
Marxist theory 9
Mascret, N. 29
mastery 7, 14, 19, 96
mastery experiences 13
Mata, A. 28
mathematics: ability and, implicit theories about 25–26, 29; inclusion and 36, 40, 42, 46; programming and 60
medical model 8–9
medical perspective 3
memorisation strategies 38
Merton, Robert *see* self-fulfilling phrophecies
metacognitive ability 104, 145
Mitchell, David 35, 38
morphemes 112–116; bound 112–113; compound words 113–114, 116, 118, 119, 120; derivational 113; free 112–113; grammatical 113, 114, 119; prefixes 113, 114, 115, 116–117, 120; root 112–113; suffixes 113, 114, 115, 116–117, 118, 119, 120, 121
morphological skills 112, 113, 114
morphology 112–122; intervention programme and, setting up 116–122; morphological skills and reading development 114–116; morphological structure and 112–114; summary 122; *see also* morphemes
mother tongue 103, 106, 107
motivation: digital narratives and 56; film, visuals, and creative writing and 92, 96; growth mindsets and 4–5; implicit theories of ability and 24–25, 26, 29, 30; importance of 108, 109–110; meaningfulness and 108; programming and 60; of staff 34; Tistedal inclusion project and 34, 36, 37
motor skills 136
multisensory approach 44, 47, 50

National Literacy Trust 63–64
Norway: morphological awareness study in 114, 118; teachers' self-efficacy in, influence of 16
Norwegian school *see* Tistedal primary school
Norwegian Teacher Self-Efficacy Scale (NTSES) 12

Ohler, J. B. 55
optimistic beliefs 1; Bandura and 4, 8, 11, 16; of overcoming difficulties 8; self-efficacy and 11, 16; Seligman and 3; student well-being and 3–4
oral language 141, 145, 147; morphological awareness and 118; mother tongue and 103, 106, 107; Witting method and 140, 146, 148; written language differentiated from 146

participation: Attention Autism to support 48; community activities to support 19; electoral 17; Tistedal inclusion project to support 36; visual literacy to support 87, 90, 96; visual stimuli to support 100; Witting method to support 140
pedagogy: in leadership 106; learning intentions and 47; models permeated with 7; positive approach to 49; tool 54–55
"People Who Help" 64–65
persuasion 7, 14, 19, 20
pessimistic beliefs 8
Pete The Cat I love my white shoes (Litwen) 49
phonemes 105

phonics 47–48, 125, 127, 129
physical active learning: categorising students and 27; digital tools and 54; in EHCP, at Archdale School 46; QR codes and 58; Tistedal inclusion project and 32, 42
physiological states 14
Pippi Longstocking 113–114
positive education *see* positive special education
positive psychology: learned helplessness and 2, 4; learned optimism and 2, 3; positive special education inspired by 1; *see also* positive special education
positive special education: described 1–2; digital tools and 54–61; growth mindsets and 4–5; inclusive literacy and 85–95; learned helplessness and 2; learned optimism and 3; misconception about 1; morphological structures of words and 112–122; optimistic beliefs and 3–4; positive psychology perspective and 1, 2–3; reading and writing without fixed material 103–110; research on 1; self-efficacy and 4, 7–20; SEND schools and 63–72, 131; sense of coherence and 4; student well-being and 3–4; Tistedal inclusion project and 32–43; Witting Method and 139–148
Positiv Specialpedagogik: Teorier och tillämpningar 110
predictive skills 98
prejudice 10, 11
preschool: morphological awareness training in 114–116; reading environments in 104; reading to children in 146; words to introduce in 116–117, 120
problem-solving skills 38, 83
programming 59–61; colours 60–61; mathematical concepts 60; recipes 61; skills 61; Swedish 61; words and concepts 59–60
props 50, 55, 64–65; in Archdale School lesson plan 50; in digital narrative 55; sensory, in digital narrative 64–65

QR codes, quiz walks with 58
questionnaires for measuring self-efficacy 12–13
quiz walks with QR codes 58

Rattan, A. 29
reading comprehension 105–107
reading skills: differentiated teaching and 131; inclusive literacy and 85, 89, 90; QR codes and 58; text to develop 124; visuals and film to support 96; vocabulary knowledge and 112–122; Witting method and 139–148
reasoning skills 87
Reichenberg, Monica 3, 5, 36, 58, 87, 105, 112, 148
right-based model 18, 20n1; *see also* capability approach
Robinson model 34, *34*
robots 60–61
Room on the Broom (Donaldson) 124–129
root morphemes 112–113
Rosenberg, M. 13

scaffolding: descriptive writing and 94; for development of different abilities 56; language supports and 48; text to develop literacy and 130
scales for measuring self-efficacy 12–13
SCERTS 46, 50
science: digital narratives and 55, 56; notions of ability as fixed and 26
Sefton-Green, J. 58
self-confidence 27, 90, 108, 109, 145
self-efficacy: beneficial consequences of, on teachers' work 14–15; collective 12; growth mindsets and 4–5; importance of, in positive special education 4; measuring, with scales and questionnaires 12–13; Skaalvik and Skaalvik and 12; skills 11, 13; sources influencing extent of 13–14; of students, teachers' support of development of 16; of teachers, influencing teaching and outcomes of civic education 16–17; of teachers, influencing teaching in functional literacy 17–19; *see also* Bandura, Albert
self-esteem 3, 13, 57, 108, 109, 130
self-fulfilling phrophecies 15, 27
self-persuasion 20
Seligman, Martin: learned helplessness and 2, 4; learned optimism and 2, 3; optimistic beliefs and 3; pessimistic beliefs and 8; positive psychology and 2–3

semantic bootstrapping 117
Semi-Formal Curriculum 63
SEND (Special Educational Needs and Disabilities) 63–72, 131
sense of coherence, Antonovsky's 4, 54, 108
senses in Witting method, multiple 148
Shanahan, T. 106
Shipton, Catherine 55
Simple View of Reading 144
Skaalvik, E. M. and S, self-efficacy and 12
skills: Attention Autism and 48; cognitive 131, 135; communication (*see* communication skills); comprehension 96, 100; core learning and 47; grammatical 124; ICT 75; implicit notions of ability and 23; independent 72, 98; life 3, 96; map 60; morphological 112, 113, 114; motor 136; phonic 127, 129; problem-solving 38, 83; programming 61; reading (*see* reading skills); reasoning 87; self-efficacy 11, 13; social (*see* social skills); speaking and listening (*see* speaking and listening skills); spelling 113; teaching 13, 15, 35; underestimation of, medical model and 8; understanding and predictive 98; writing (*see* writing skills)
Snow, Catherine, Word Generation and 118
social cognitive theory 4, 11
social model 9–10; social constuctivist 9; Nordic/relational 9; Marxist 9
social skills 32, 33, 38, 96, 132
socioeconomically disadvantaged 10
sociology 12
speaking and listening skills: inclusive literacy and 85, 87; pupils with SEN and 74, 81; visuals and film to support 98
special education *see* positive special education
special educational needs: Attention Autism and 48–49, 65, 71, 72; differentiated teaching, at Swiss Cottage School 131–138; positive (*see* positive special education); teachers' self-efficacy and 13; teaching expressive communication to pupils with SEND 63–72, 131; teaching functional literacy to pupils with SEN 74–84; teaching literacy to children with, in special schools in England 44–52
speech synthesis 54–55
spelling skills 113
spoken language *see* oral language
stable success factors 2, 3
station work 38, *39*, 39–40
Steimer, A. 28
stereotypes 9, 10, 11, 26–27
stigmatisation 10, 11
student learning responsibility 145
Swärd, Ann-Katrin 38, 54, 57, 59, 87, 104, 109, 140, 141, 143, 145, 146
Sweden 9, 17; ability and 26; compulsory education for children/youths with ID in 9; digital tools and 55, 56, 58, 59; electoral participation in 17; influence of teachers' self-efficacy 16–19; QR codes and 58; Swedish words and language 61, 103, 141, 144
Swedish Government Decision (2018) U2018/01430/S 58
Swiss Cottage School Model 5, 18, 75, 131–138; class context and lesson structure 131–132; learning intentions 132–137; plenary 137–138; Travel Training 74–84
symbol function: in content neutral language structures 145; described 105; in reading and writing processes 143–144; turning language sounds into symbols 146–147

Tang, X. 108–109
Teachers' Standards, in England and Wales 64
teacher standard 5 (TS5) 64
teaching skills 13, 15, 35
Tistedal primary school 32–43; *see also* inclusive education
transportation, independence in 17–19, 74–84
Tunmer, W. E. 144

understanding skills 98

Vägledning i det praktiska metodarbetet (Guidance in the practical methodological work) (Witting) 139–140
verbal persuasion 14

verbal presentation through an avatar 56
vicarious experiences 14, 19
virtual reality (VR) 58–59
visual literacy: inclusive literacy and 85–95; learning outcomes 100–102; lesson in 96–100; using visuals and film to support literacy 96–102; *see also* inclusive literacy
vocabulary: academic 115, 116, 118; core vocabulary board and 47, 48, 51; Creative Word Search and 143; linguistic awareness and 104; questioning for developing 87; in teaching expressive communication to pupils with SEND 65; text to develop 124, 127; training 121; virtually experiencing words for understanding 59; visuals and film to support 98; words based on experience and 146; *see also* morphemes; morphological skills
voting 16–17

Walker, Melanie 122
What Really Works in Special and Inclusive Education (Mitchell) 38
Witting, Maja 104, 105, 139–148; *see also* Witting method
Witting method 139–148; ability, know and trust your own 148; additional goals in 147–148; Attentive Writing in 140–141, 143, 144, 145, 147–148; classroom work in 140–143; comprehension/content creation in 144; content-neutral language structures in 105, 110, 139, 144–145, 148; Creative Word Search in 140, 141–143, 144, 145, 147, 148; independence work in 145; language sounds in 146; linguistic awareness in 147; multiple senses in, use of 148; preparatory work in 145–146; reading and writing processes in 139, 143–144; student learning responsibility in 145; symbol function in 105, 143–147; teacher comments on working with 148; turning language sounds into symbols in 146–147; words based on experience in, need for 146; written language differs from oral language in 146
Wittingmetodens idébakgrund (Idea background of the Witting method) (Witting) 139–140
Wood, D. 56
Word Generation 118
words *see* vocabulary
World Health Organization (WHO) 8
Wramner, L. 59, 143
writing skills: Attentive Writing 140–141, 143, 144, 145, 147–148; descriptive 93–94; different dimensions of writing and 106–107; differentiated teaching and 131; digital tools for 54, 55, 57; inclusive literacy and 85, 89; pupils with SEND and 72; text to develop 124; Witting method and 139–148
written language: linguistic awareness and 104; morphological awareness and 118; oral language differentiated from 146; reading comprehension and 105, 107; vocabulary teaching and 122; Witting method and 139, 143–144

Yeager, D. S. 27

For Product Safety Concerns and Information please contact our EU representative GPSR@taylorandfrancis.com
Taylor & Francis Verlag GmbH, Kaufingerstraße 24, 80331 München, Germany

www.ingramcontent.com/pod-product-compliance
Lightning Source LLC
Chambersburg PA
CBHW051542230426
43669CB00015B/2695